THE MOMENT OF CHANGE

THE MOMENT OF CHANGE

An Anthology of Feminist Speculative Poetry
edited by Rose Lemberg

Published by Aqueduct Press
PO Box 95787
Seattle, WA 98145-2787
www.aqueductpress.com

Publishing histories provided in Acknowledgements.

First Printing, May 2012
10 9 8 7 6 5 4 3 2 1

ISBN: 978-1-61976-006-6

Library of Congress Control Number: 2012935514

Cover illustrations courtesy Terri Windling
Front cover: The Spirit of Sabino Canyon
Back cover: Detail from The Spirit of Air
www.terriwindling.com

Book Design by Kathryn Wilham

Printed in the USA by Applied Digital Imaging

Contents

Introduction

Rose Lemberg

the mind of the poet is the only poem [...]
the mind of the poet is changing
the moment of change is the only poem.

> (Adrienne Rich, "Images for Godard,"
> from *The Will to Change*)

We seek out change to dream ourselves into the world. But even though we are in the world, our voices are folded into the creases. We speak from memory of stories told sidewise. We speak from pain; is that serious enough? The world has not been welcoming, but what other world is there?

Literature of the fantastic allows us to create worlds and visions of society, origins, social justice, and identity. As such, it is directly relevant to feminism; and of all the genres of speculative literature, poetry is crucial. In the words of Audre Lorde,

> For women, then, poetry is not a luxury. It is a vital
> necessity of our existence. [...] Poetry is the way we
> help give name to the nameless so it can be thought.
> The farthest external horizons of our hopes and
> fears are cobbled by our poems, carved from the rock
> experiences of our daily lives.[1]

But it is not enough for our voices to simply exist; poets writing from marginalized perspectives must also find venues sympathetic to their work, spaces in which to be heard and engage with their readership. And yet, conversations about speculative feminist poetry have been frustratingly rare, even though major figures have pioneered the field and produced powerful work.

The mythic poetry movement has been central to the emerging body of diverse feminist engagement in a field previously dominated by other perspectives. Terri Windling and Midori Snyder's *Journal of the Mythic Arts* published poetry and articles with a strong feminist bent; Amal El-Mohtar and Jessica Paige Wick, editors of *Goblin Fruit*, contributed to the maturation of the movement by providing an explicitly feminist outlet for mythic and folkloric work; Mike Allen, the editor of *Mythic Delirium* and Mythic anthologies, showcased multiple perspectives, including but not limited to feminist poetry. In the late 2000s, the mythic poetry movement truly came into its own; poets working in this tradition won the Rhysling Award with diverse feminist work.

And yet, conversations within the field of speculative poetry have often downplayed or ignored these voices, while claiming that diversity in the speculative realm is rare to nonexistent.

In Summer 2010, I started a new venue, *Stone Telling* (now co-edited with my partner in crime, Shweta Narayan). I wanted to showcase diverse voices and multiple perspectives not just in the mythic tradition, but across genres. Setting out, I was curious as to what has been already done in the field vis-a-vis representing the voices and narratives of women and outsiders. I found multiple anthologies of speculative poetry, but not a single one labeled itself feminist, or even focused on women's creativity in this domain. A vast majority of these anthologies have been edited by men.

I did find the brilliant *Women of Other Worlds*, a feminist anthology which came out in 1999; the mission of the editors Helen Merrick and Tess Williams is in many ways aligned with my own stated interest in fostering "empowerment through valuing diverse, often marginalized voices." However, the anthology features only two poems (both of which are reprinted in these pages). I wanted to find out if there's been more, to find out for myself if it's true what they say, that the field of speculative poetry is just not diverse: live with it, accept it, move on. But I knew of poems and poets that defied this; certainly I could find more, published here and there, in the field and out of it. Thus the idea for *The Moment of Change* was born.

When L. Timmel Duchamp agreed to publish the anthology, I announced an open submissions period, asked people for recommendations, talked to poets and editors, and read through the archives of multiple magazines and anthologies. My conclusion? Yes, there is diversity in speculative poetry. What we were lacking was a space in which to have a conversation, a space in which our diverse voices could resonate against each other and create an amplified and complex meaning.

The collection is before you: a roadmap to what diverse, intersectional feminist speculative poetry is and what it can become.

In these pages you will find works in a variety of genres—works that can be labeled mythic, fantastic, science fictional, historical, surreal, magic realist, and unclassifiable; poems by people of color and white folks; by poets based in the US, Canada, Britain, India, Spain, and the Philippines; by first- and second-generation immigrants; by the able-bodied and the disabled; by straight and queer poets who may identify as women, men, trans, and genderqueer. Some of the authors also write fiction, creative non-fiction, and academic scholarship; others focus solely on poetry. Some of the authors are established, others emerging. Some identify primarily as literary poets, others as speculative poets. Their ages range from early twenties to eighties. As Flavia Dzodan says, "My feminism will be intersectional or it will be bullshit."

I think of this collection as a cornerstone—a compendium of dreams, oppressions, hopes, empowerment, yearning, and mature strength that comes from knowing that we are here. We speak with voices that have been silenced, ignored, marginalized, suppressed, ridiculed, forgotten. We re-remember ourselves, constantly remake ourselves, grapple with theory and life's challenges. "See us," the poets of this collection say. "Change with us. Walk with us. Dream with us."

We are not monolithic. We argue, often bitterly, between ourselves. We disagree, and we create works of power and beauty that arise from these disagreements. We congregate in communities or work alone, but we are no longer invisible. By seeing each other, by empowering each other, we reimagine the world, re-narrate society and history, celebrate our voices and complex identities through the filter of speculative creativity.

We are here.

Note

1   "Poetry Is Not a Luxury," *Sister Outsider: Essays and Speeches.* Crossing Press, 1984

Werewomen

Ursula K. Le Guin

I want to go moonwalking
on it or under it I don't care
I just want to go moonwalking
alone.
Women in their sixties
don't go to the moon,
women in the cities
don't go out alone.
But I want O listen what I want
is to be not afraid.
Listen what I need is freedom.
Women in their sixties
think about dying,
all kinds of women
think about lying,
think about lying alone.
But listen there's a moon out there
and I don't want sex and I don't want death
and I don't want what you think I want,
only to be a free woman.
What is that, a free woman,
a young free woman,
an old free woman?
Asking for the moon.
Women in their sixties
have no moon.
Women in the cities
howl at the moon.
All kinds of women

talk about walking alone.
When the moon is full
listen how they howl,
listen how they howl together.

Harvest Season

Nicole Kornher-Stace

Between them all, the children
recognize perhaps five written letters
from their native tongue; not one
can spell her name — and yet
with voices older than their flesh they sing
the culling-songs, unwinding-songs,
fleet-fingered songs: one hoarse-voiced
where the ivy had once reached green fingers
round her throat and snugged up
to the bright fire of her breath (in a whirl of blades
they'd rescued her, but the scars stay); another with
a mangled knife-hand where a tendril,
in an eyeblink, grew clean through.
Their native tongue's obliterate. Their cradle tongue
is bones. Each with her apple-basket,
milk-pail, apron-front, they gather yellowed skulls,
some whole (why, the better to drink your health
from!), most deconstructed in the grasp
of vines and time to orbits,
frontals, maxillae — mosaic tesserae
destined for a rose window, a breastplate,
an intarsia-topped gueridon, a clutch of poison rings.
Their pockets stuffed with metatarsals,
eyeteeth, vertebrae (hedgewitch runestones,
swordhilt fripperies and prayer-beads), they braid
the useless fragments through their greasy hair
with fingers swollen from the wrenchings
where the slick green leaves
fight back. They sing, but not to keep
from weeping: where nice little girls hoard

dolls and seashells, they hoard tales, gaze up
through the green, and know
that every ruined tower has its princess —
and a harp pieced of her royal bones
might buy them passage
to the sea.

Prayer

Eliza Victoria

A tree sits in the wasteland of my mother's memory. The tree faces a river in her hometown, on the shore where nothing else grows. Like a curious child, it sits watching the boat that approaches it tonight, with the moon full and the stars slowly disappearing behind clouds like gossiping neighbors. On the boat is a sow, squealing like a prisoner. Someone lives in the tree. The tree-owner has many faces, hiding behind a window, in the crowd at the market, in the shadow of your bed. The sow is payment for a request, and the tree-owner always answers with an empty boat, floating down the river back to its sender.

How innocent the tree must look in the morning, like breakfast, like ourselves in that cold hour when we are lost in someone else's limbs, and we have yet to think of sacrifices. In a dark room, a mother-to-be sees blood between her thighs, and her husband runs out with a bolo, urging the shadows to face him like a man. This is not a death; this is an empty boat bobbing on tiny waves, a sow squealing itself to silence, an enemy masterminding his grief. The tree is useful that way, when you are blind with rage or fear, when you need to trace causality. How random is loss, and how we ache to have someone to blame, or to keep us safe. In any given time in this city, a sacrifice skids across the concrete sea, wraps itself around a tree that dares stand in the way. I send a sow across the river for the safety of everyone I love, and wait for the boat to return.

Cave-Smell

Shweta Narayan

My mother was a brown bear
honey-lover, heavy paw
cave-smelling warm

You say I am a girl
though my fur hangs heavy
and my claws click, stumbling careful
on your keyboard

You smelled breath and fur
leavings and closed spaces
set me down, backed away
tranq gun raised

I ask: <<What will I be?>>
A celebrity, you say. A triumph of neuroscience
and philanthropy.

Words too long to type. I say: <<No,
go to school.>>
You laugh and pet me.
Bright girl, brown girl,
bears don't do that.

I smelled home
but she worried that implant plate with her rough tongue
licked shaved skin raw

and if she spoke
I did not know the words.

And there's a laugh in your smile
when I eat honey or sashimi
And fear in your anger
when I snarl

though you do these things too.

When you called
in my new tongue
I did not look back at her

So I click, heavy-clawed
and write my halting
small-word
cave-smell stories
in the tongue you taught

And wonder if my daughters will read them
or if they will be brown bears.

The Witch

Theodora Goss

Sometimes in the morning, the mist curled into the corners
Of the house like a cat, and Grimalkin, she would cry,
come to me, my Grimalkin. She would gather
the mist to her, and stroke it, and it would settle
in her lap, and lick itself.

Sometimes, she wove
cobwebs and out of the cloth, thin, gray, luminescent,
she would cut the pattern for a dress. But for what purpose?
Where could she wear it? Where could she go, except
to the pond, where she would kneel and dip her fingers
into the water, and stir, and out would jump
a trout, thick, silver, luminescent, and splashing
water onto her dress, whose hem was already
soaked and covered with mud.

She would make it speak,
recite Shakespearean sonnets, sing old songs,
before she put it into the pot. Witches
are lonely, but also hungry, and practical
in their impracticality. She had learned
how from her mother, the old witch, now dead
if witches are ever entirely dead, which is doubtful.

She never wondered who her father had been,
a peasant gathering wood, perhaps a hunter,
perhaps even a prince, on his way to the country
where a princess had been promised for dispatching
a dragon or something similar, and had seen
a light through the trees, and found her mother waiting,
and perhaps gone on the next morning, and perhaps not.

Her mother had built the house by the edge of the pond,
out of gray stone and branches of white birch,
birds' nests and moss, and spit to hold it together.
That is how witches build what they call houses.
What they are not: sturdy, comfortable.
What they are: cold.

There was still a row of bottles
in the cupboard, holding martens' eyes, dried frogs,
robins' eggs, random feathers, balls of string,
oak galls. She had forgotten what they were for.
From the rafters hung a fox's skeleton.

Once, village girls had come to visit her mother
for charms to attract the schoolmaster's attention,
make their rivals' hair fall out, abortions.

Afterward, they would say, Did you see her? Standing
by the door? In her ragged dress, with her tangled hair,
I tell you, she creeps me out. But they stopped coming
after the old witch disappeared and her daughter
was left alone. Sometimes she would remember
the smell of the bread in their pockets, the clink of coins,
their dresses covered with embroidery,
their whispering, and look at her reflection
in the pond, floating on the water like a ghost.

Sometimes she made the frogs at the edge of the pond,
calling to one another, speak to her.
"Pretty one," they would say, "in your spider silk,
in your birchbark shoes, like a princess lost in the woods,
kiss us." But she knew that was not her story.

Sometimes she would make the birds perch on her fingers
and sing to her: warblers, thrushes, chickadees,
and sing to them out of tune, then break their necks
and roast them.

Sometimes she would gather the stones
that had fallen from her house, and think of making
a dog, a stone dog. Then, she would forget.
It was the forgetting that made her what she was,
her mother's daughter. Witches never remember
important things: that fire burns, and that bottles
labeled poison are not to be drunk. Witches
are always doing what they should not, dancing
at midnight with the Gentleman, kicking their skirts
over the tops of their stockings, kissing frogs
they know perfectly well won't turn into princes.

She makes no magic. Although the stories won't tell you,
witches are magic. They do not need the props
of a magician, the costumes or the cards,
the scarves, the rabbits. They came down from the moon
originally, and it still calls to them,
so they go out at night, when the moon is shining,
and make no magic, but magic happens around them.

Sometimes at night she would look up at the moon
and call Mother? Mother? but never got an answer.

I want you to imagine: her ragged dress,
her hair like cobwebs, her luminescent eyes,
mad as all witches are, stirring the pond
like a cauldron (witches need no cauldrons, whatever
the stories tell you) while above her the clouds
are roiling and a storm is about to gather.

On the Division of Labour

Amal El-Mohtar

They say, they,
(whose lips keep moist by many means)
that only men may brandish
such a fierce instrument. Stripped yew, strung
with mute gut — a hoarseness culled
from teeth-ground groans and bloody sweat —
its music's fit for furies' ears,
but not for ladies.

A lady's hands, they say,
are not rough enough; a lady's eye
too soft
to slice distance into
a bloody wound in the thigh. True enough.

The ladies
must needs smile; turn their sights
away from manly pursuits, drop their gazes instead
to the needles in their laps; the threads;
the scissors poised to cut.

The Birth of Science Fiction

J. C. Runolfson

Mother Mary gasps and twists in her labor,
it's so hot in this country,
the storm coming.
When the angel came, she should have chased it out
with green fairy lewdness.
She is no god's handmaiden
and she would not have done this for a god.
Only her mother, spreading ghost-wings in her,
speaking the words, "To be a good mother — a woman
must have sense, and that independence of mind
which few women possess who are taught to depend
entirely on their husbands."
That is no trouble here. Her husband barely has anything to do
with issue that is his, and this is certainly not his.
Perhaps if he's away from it, it will survive.
So Mary labors alone, throws the windows open to the rain.
Yanks the sheets from the bed, catches up foolscap and pen.
She writes in a frenzy in that chateau,
and Percy screams over eyes in her nipples,
but she has been screaming since their first child died
and he still doesn't hear.
She leaves him to Byron, a master of distractions
in her time of focus, her hours of work,
the holy words.
Blessed Mary, pretty little Mary,
"is woman in a natural state?"
"I am alone and miserable."
She's given birth before, but this is a special child.

This is an immortal child, the one to survive
when she joins her mother and her daughter,
the one she has built of all the most beautiful
and terrible parts of herself.
This is the child of angel and ghost.
Mother Mary gives one last great push
as darkness falls, as the storm descends.
When the lightning strikes, she knows it's alive.

Resurrection of a Pin Doll

Kristine Ong Muslim

I prod her to stay awake,
threaten to throw her into
the toy box where the warrior
boy with the bayonet resides.

Her button eyes begin to take on
a hint of color, a darker brown like
the eyes of the missing neighborhood girl.

This is my lovely pin doll
stuffed with the softest of innards.

Each day a pin pierces her heart.
Each day a pin punctures her lung.
She sings all the time.

Kristallnacht

Lawrence Schimel

She wore glass spectacles
for her vision was clouded,
as if that night her family's home
was burned to the ground in a pogrom
the smoke had gotten into her eyes
and never left them.

They named her Cinderella
when they pulled her from the ashes,
their hearts going soft because
she was only three years old.
Years later, her stepsisters teased
that she was named Cinderella
because she was dark as soot.
They pinched her bold nose
and pulled her black hair
and powdered their pale faces
to go to parties with the Viennese elite.

Cinderella was never invited
to attend these lavish functions;
her foster family left her at home,
working while they danced,
dreaming of the day she was asked to accompany them.
She was always certain it would not be long,
and therefore worked unfailingly, hoping
for approval.

While her stepsisters primped and prepped
to waltz among princes, Cinderella walked

to the market, stepping over sewage in the gutters,
dodging the nimble rats that boldly crossed
the streets in search of food. A kindly frau
who sat beside a cart of squash — yellow gourds
and fat pumpkins like lumpy little suns — stopped her.
She took Cinderella's hands into her own.
"You look so sad. I will help you."
The woman drew Cinderella into the shadows
of the alleyway, and pulled papers from her pocket.
"Take these," she said. "They are mine,
but I am old. Go to America instead of me.
Find a new life. Send for your family,
if any are still alive. I am too old to begin again.
But for you, there is still hope for you."

Cinderella stared at this woman. "I am
no Jew," she said, handing back the papers.
She walked away, but the frau's words —
the insinuations, the generosity —
haunted her. She walked faster,
trying to outrun the echoes in her mind.

Passing a shop window, Cinderella saw
a pair of slippers made of glass.
If she had been invited to the ball,
she thought, she would wear those.
She stared at them,
and her reflection stared back:
swart, square. Semitic.

She bought the slippers with the grocery money
and hurried back to the now-empty house.
Cinderella powdered her face
with the stepsister's cosmetics,

put on one of their dresses.
She tied her dark hair in a knot
hiding it beneath a silver scarf.
But still her nose betrayed her.
She didn't care. She slipped on her glass shoes
and made her way across town to the gala,
dreaming of finding a prince who would love her
and adore her and take her away to an enchanted life
where it did not matter that she looked like a Jew.

The party was as dazzling as she had dreamed.
No one stopped her at the door, or paid her any
notice at all, it seemed, though some people stared.
No one spoke to her. And then a shriek
made Cinderella the focus of six hundred eyes,
as her two stepsisters ran toward her.
"You are not fit to be seen here!" they cried.
They snatched the spectacles from her face
and, in front of the assembled crowd,
crushed them underfoot with a delicate
twist of the toe, grinding downward.

Cinderella's vision blurred without her glasses.
Tears burned in her eyes, and then suddenly
the smoke that had clouded her sight
for as long as she could recall
lifted. She saw, at last, what she had always
refused to see before: these people had killed
her family, had meant to kill her as well.

She stood there, numb, as the stepsisters
poked and pushed her. They stepped
on her toes and broke her glass slippers
into hundreds of sharp splinters.

Cinderella left the shards of her glass shoes
on the dance floor and walked barefoot
out of the hall, leaving footprints of blood
behind her. She was never seen again.

The Last Yangtze River Dolphin

Cassandra Phillips-Sears

"I will not wed one
I cannot love," I said.
They cried
for who I could have been
what they would not have:
obedience, grandchildren
and approving neighbors.

Grass, tall along its banks, hid:
my tears; I did not like to make them cry.
Later, my body.

I awoke in the cradle
of the water,
which no familiar, callused hands,
unless they are the moon's,
need rock: and hers never pushed me under.

Drowned princesses
a thousand thousand strong
surrounded me, singing
with their bodies
lifted me,
taught me how to swim.
My soul must have passed
through some strange heaven,
was my last thought of metaphysics.

☉

I wake up, two feet
tangled in a net
of bedclothes
and her arms,
remembering and failing.
It was a boat that killed me, this last time. Or
it was the look upon my father's face.

I try to sleep
and start to cry.

This river is so dark
I must sing to see my way.

The Stepsister

Peg Duthie

When she kissed the mirror, it burst into tears
and the drops scalded the surface of her vanity,
splashing against the bracelet of apple seeds
and the swatch of venom-infused cloak.
Never mind that all of her shoes fit
and that she kneads her own bread
to feed the wolves as well as the grandmothers:
there will be no room in the book
to spell out her side of the story.

The Girl with Two Skins

Catherynne M. Valente

I.

On your knees between moon-green shoots,
beside a sack of seed, a silver can, a white spade,
a ball is tucked into the bustle of your skirt,
like a pearl
but not a pearl. You pulled it up
round as a beet from between the mint and the beans
where I had sunk it in the earth,
as though I fished
for loam-finned, moss-gilled coelacanth
at the bottom of the world.
I thought it safe.

I crawl to you on belly henna-bright,
teeth out,
scratching the basil sprouts:
eyes flash phosphor. In the late light,
slant gold light,
you must see
the old tail echo
beneath my muddy dress:
two, three, nine.

I howl against the barking churchbells:
Give it back, give it back,
I need it.

II.

Once I skulked snoutwise through scrap-iron forests,
And to each man with his silver pail scowled:

You are not beautiful enough
to make me human.

I had a fox's education:
rich coffee grounds in every house-gutter,
mice whose bones were sweet to suck,
stolen bread and rainwater on whiskers:
slow theogonies of bottle-caps and housecats.
I crouched, the color of rusted stairs,
and to each boy who chased me
through rotted wheat laughed:

You are not beautiful enough
to turn my tail to feet!

But this is a story,
and in a story
there is always someone
beautiful enough.

In a wood I found you
in the classical way,
a girl in a dress with a high hem,
ribbons in her teeth,
honey on her thumbs.

(Damn all your red hair
just enough like fur,
Damn all your small mouth,
your damp smell,
Damn all your pianos and stitching hoops.
Had I but paws enough to stamp out
your every spoken word like snow!)

Make your waist like this,
indicating curve.
Make your eyes like this,
indicating blue.
Make your face
make your skin
make your clever, clever hands,
make them this way,
indicating civilized,
indicating soft, your own,
your freckled breast linen-bound.

The old vixens, with their scabby,
mushroom-strung claws,
only said to run from boys,
and you looked so thick and pure,
like the inside
of a bone.

III.

I lashed my tail to my waist
in your gold-wood kitchen,
ridiculous in blue silk,
with cornflowers in my ears.
We bent over squash soup and sour cherries,
you put your hands over mine
to show me how to crease dough
over a silver pan.
I bit your cheek at tea-time;
you smelled all day of my musk.

No, you laughed like sugar stirring,
your feet are too black,
your teeth are so sharp!
Can you not stand up straight

in my old dresses
can you not make your flesh
like mine?
Shamed, fur flamed across my cheek,
but you patted it pale with flour and sweet,
and I wept to be savage and bristle-stiff
in such a tidy place,
in such silent, clean arms.

I slept curled
at the foot of your bed,
reeking of lavender and lilac
though I spied no purple field.
I growled at moths that plagued your hair
and woke with every stairwell-creak.
But you brushed back my pelt
with lullabies,
into a long braid that fell
across pillows like shoulder blades.
You showed me the word *kitsune*
in a book with a long ribbonmark
like blood spilled on the print —
I chewed the page and swallowed it,
and learned there only that
crawling into your arms,
embarrassed by my heat, my wet nose,
was like becoming
a girl with two skins.

IV.

This is a story,
and it is true of all stories
that the sound when they slam shut
is like a key turning.

I was sewing, hands two bloody half-paws —
it takes such a long time to
become a woman —
smears of needle-bitten skin,
and you scrutinizing the cross-stitching:
no, no, like this, my love, like mine —
when he came to call, when you
with hair sleek as linseed oil
and my eyes still so black,
still unable to imitate the blue you demanded,
danced with him in our kitchen,
fed him our yellow soups with sprigs of thyme.
He smiled at me, with pomade in that grin,
and walking canes, and silverware,
and spring gloves. I snapped at him,
for a simple fox may still understand her rival,
and know what is expected.

But the recoil! The shrieking of her
the shrinking into his great smooth arms,
the lifting of her blue skirts to keep them clear
of the stink of my fume!

A vixen chews out the throat of her enemies
like stripping bark from a birch;
it is the sophisticated thing.
How was I to know you meant to keep him?

Absurd in my torn dress,
tail bulging free, the muzzle
you tried so to train to lips,
curled back, knife-whiskered,
I stood with blood beating my flesh to drum-taut,
in our kitchen, in our hall,
mange-sodden and mud-bellied,
before the man who was

beautiful enough,
beautiful enough.

V.

It is not possible, you said later,
when I scrabbled at the door he built,
when my skin was blue and bruised,
and there was no russet left in me,
when my nakedness in the snow
was goosepimpled and smelled so damp,
so much like soup
and cherries
and creased dough in a silver pan —
it is not possible to love for long
what is not a girl, sweet nor soft,
nor civilized,
nor trained to tile and mantle-shine,
stray beast in the house,
scolded when she spoils supper
with her hunger,
when her rough tongue spoils
every cultivated thing,
skin and sewing and lavender bed together.

See how tall he stands.
See how gentle his voice.
See how his hands on me never cut.

Then give it back,
I need it,
my pearl
which is not a pearl.
I do not want your shape.
Let me go back
I want to go back.

But you keep it by you,
pretty jeweled thing,
it adorns you as I did not.
The heat of you
warms it like an egg.

I am cold in the evening of blue warnings,
I haunt your garden,
your raspberry rows,
your squash blossoms,
a naked wastrel,
flat teeth chattering.
I hold one arm out to you,
clung with snail-tracked ruin,
keep one over my breasts,
which you taught to be modest.

As the moon comes up
like a pearl,
but not a pearl,
you gather up the mint and rosemary,
and do not see
how I claw with woman's nails
the waist you gave me,
just to make it red again.

Binnorie

Theodora Goss

What is it about being made into a harp,
Your bones as smooth as poplar, about being strung
With your own hair, golden or black or brown,
That presents such an appropriate allegory
For being a woman, and therefore an instrument
Of fathers, husbands, or sons? Or is it rather
An allegory for being a poet, which is
A different thing altogether, I like to think,
Although poetry can command you like a father,
Berate you like a husband, and abandon
You like any number of sons?

Learning to Locate Colors in Grey:
Kiran Talks About Her Brothers

Nandini Dhar

(After the classic Bengali fairytale Arun-Barun-Kiranmala compiled by Dakshinaranjan Mitra Majumder in his Thakumar Jhuli [Tales from Granny's Bag]. Kiranmala or Kiran is one of the protagonists of the tale, who, in order to take care of herself and her brothers, Arun and Barun, dresses up as a man and defeats the demons successfully.)

I heard many more stories than those contained in the following pages;
but I rejected a great many, as they appeared to me to contain spurious
additions to the original stories which I had heard when a boy. I have
reason to believe that the stories given in this book are a genuine
sample of the old old stories told by old Bengali women from age to
age through a hundred generations.
— Lal Behari Dey, *Preface to Folktales of Bengal*

Her father never knew her
or her brothers' birthmarks.

He wasn't there to witness them.

They had come to him, in coconut-leaf dinghies,
knifing the river like quick cutlasses.

A fact she didn't know until later.

He (who she calls her father) takes refuge
in a language which has ceased to exist anywhere
except in pages.
He demands

her brothers learn the script down to its last detail.
As if, those boys were indeed his own.

She, her father sets to glaze smooth shine
          her brothers' ink pots,
clean sharp the tips of their nibs.

          She possesses the advantage
            of an intimate knowledge
that she is too thick for the narrow sleekness
of their quill tips.

She finds nothing in her brothers to mimic. They cling on to an orderliness
which escapes her tongue.

          Unlike her, they see nothing other than
black and white in grey.

She has learned to locate

the teal, indigo, fuchsia, and vermilion in any measured mixture
          of ivory and slate.

Nonetheless, she knows the grey like the lines of her hand.

In and out. Out and in.

That's how she knows she will be a storyteller
and her brothers, commentators at best.

River of Silk

Rachel Manija Brown

Rough hands jerk at Draupadi's sari,
spinning her like a chariot wheel.
She closes her eyes
the only one who does
though some cannot see
and some refuse to see.
Some lean forward to see better
and smile.

Her husbands bear witness
in impotent guilt
in red-eyed fury
in cool anticipation of revenge
in sorrow
in compassion
but witness only.

Her cry arrows to its target
in a golden palace
on an island city.
Dushasana pulls and pulls
and pulls and pulls and pulls
and pulls and pulls and
her sari piles up on the marble
a river of silk with tributaries
eddies, stills, and streams.

Duryodhana looks and sees
a pool that is a floor
a floor that is a pool
a woman's laughter

a man's burning shame
quenched in deep waters
closing over his head.

Karna looks and sees
a baby in a river
a mother's face
a mother's love
the water ripples
the image shifts
to a baby in a river
a mother's face
a mother's love
for another son
and in the track of a wheel
a runnel of muddy water.

Arjuna looks and sees
trembling in reflection
the eye of a fish
and nothing more.

In a golden palace
on an island city
even Krishna looks and sees
the ocean rise up
and drown his land
before he turns his gaze back
to his beautiful Rukmini
and his flute.
He is not disturbed.
He already knows.

Draupadi opens her eyes
and looks and sees

the river of blood
that will flow for this
the blood Bhima will drink
the blood in which
she will wash her hair
the blood of the Kauravas
the blood of her husbands
and her sons
and of Uttara's labor.
She is satisfied.

She will wear a plain sari
into exile in the forest.
This fine cloth will be gathered up
and given to the poor
and every woman who wears it
will dream of blood and water.

The King's Daughters

JoSelle Vanderhooft

Of course, Papa always loves the youngest
better than his flinty kingdom, best of all.
That is the way of graying kings; their favorite
sweeps daylight up in her untangled hair, steps lilies
and forsythia through this looming grey
wasteland we call both heath and hearth.
Such gold girls have a legendary grace,
a good enchantment, almost, in their bones.

But this is not an elder sister's way,
not the way of Goneril and Regan who were yoke-
born like a double egg, snake-tailed, crow claw, red
fang and sulfurous as a Sybil's pit, rotten
in the way all daughters are when they lack favor. Our fish eyes
peered high over rosewood banisters, low beneath
the spine-curved chairs as Papa fussed,
as Papa spoiled like curdled cream:
Yes, my Cordelia my love-apple, my jewel, step
high through the heather-banked streams, plait your dawn hair
and throw your silver comb upon the chert
to raise the myrtle and dogwood back to life.
Yes, my diamond,
just like that,
my darling chuck,
my little fool.

For her, then, all the flowers, all the honey
but for her crawling sisters only wax,
the waning moon and all night-rotting things.

Of course, that is the way the story goes: the ugly turn
like milk, grow sour as fig trees dropping vinegar
all because Papa did not love them well enough
for apples and for pies.

Of course, the story never tells how Papa
tries: his hands sweaty in their palms at mother's funeral; his arm
Unsteady as he leads them to the altar; the toasts
He makes at every Yuletide absence; the heavy nights
he spins beneath his shroud-like sheet, recalling
word and glance, each time he frowned,
each time he could have smiled.
In dreams he offers them a kingdom each,
his arms held open like the world raveling
into skin, to cloth, at last to empty air
as if to say *come, my lovelies,*
come my mourning doves,
let all be forgotten.

The story never tells how hateful daughters
wish: the way their unbound ringlets ache for brushes; the fall-down
scabs gracing their knees kiss-red, untended; smiles
they mold from grimaces and tears; platitudes, at last,
so hemlock-stinging sweet on bloodless lips,
so well-rehearsed, they might as well be lies:
Oh, my noble father
more than eye can see and tongue can tell,
more even than the bounteous sea can swell
do I love you.

Of course, the story never tells these things.
We cannot talk of fathers fallible
as they are frail, of daughters sad
as they are terrible. Instead, we speak of quarterings,
betrayals, wasting madness and cold marriages.

Like rustling leaves these whine at last to dust
in favor of those tales comfortable and beloved as
the youngest girl Papa loved best,
his poppet and his jewel.

Perhaps this is why we always come to grief:
Cordelia twisting in the air like rags,
her wicked sisters strangled on knife and henbane,
the motley King exiled and world-broken
upon cold clay, beneath the brewing storms.

The Haunted Girl

Lisa Bradley

I.

The haunted girl wears white
sometimes gray
    if it's been a long time
    if the rats have been gnawing the hem
    eating the lace
sometimes her dress looks blue
    by moonlight
    tv light
sometimes it flashes silver
    another warning in the night
    reflecting your headlights.

II.

The haunted girl wears a dress
sometimes a taffeta straitjacket
    choking her from throat to calf
sometimes starched calico
    cuffs tight, waistline sharp
    like concertina wire
sometimes her dress is loose and flowing
    the cotton nearly transparent
    the weave wavering before your will
    filmy as the breath flowing from your lips
but not hers.

III.

The haunted girl has no feet.

Men don't look that far down.

IV.

The haunted girl is only sometimes a girl
sometimes she's a young woman
sometimes she's a mother
  although a murdering one.
But the haunted girl is never old.

Then she would be the crone.

V.

The haunted girl has mirror eyes
sometimes opalescent
  if you fear forgetting, being forgotten
  like barren eggshells
  empty seashells
  flashlights in the fog.
Sometimes they're black gloss
  if you fear futility
  absolute as a mine shaft
  blank as a brick wall.
Sometimes they're simply scarlet.

Because you know you have it coming.

VI.

The haunted girl is dirty
The haunted girl is clean

The haunted girl is clean
    until she is dirty
    until you realize
    you're embracing a corpse.

VII.

The haunted girl has no belly
    only a cave beneath her ribs
The haunted girl has a bikini belly
    carved with muscle useless
    but for pin-up poses and celluloid dreams
The haunted girl has a gently swelling belly
    soft and welcoming
    ready to absorb you
    ready to birth
    an array of monsters.

VIII.

The haunted girl has a cunt
a multiplicity of cunts
too many to describe.

IX.

The haunted girl chokes out her truth
The haunted girl tells lies
The haunted girl singsongs or grunts
Just depends on how she died
    did they cut out her tongue?
    did they crush her vocal cords?
    did they slit her throat?
    did they stab her lungs?

Does she have a secret to tell?
>would you even listen?

X.

The haunted girl is always cold
sometimes she grips you
>icy fingers on your sweaty skin
sometimes she slides against you
>a porcelain princess
>caressed but never cherished
sometimes she is a breath of midnight
>the mausoleum whisper kissing your neck.

XI.

The haunted girl is always cold
I know — I have tried to warm her
I've wrapped my coat around her shoulders
I've tied a scarf beneath her chin
I've seated her beside the skittish fire
>given her hot mugs she cannot hold
I've tried to run a warm bath
I've tried to change her clothes
I've torn the white gray blue dirty clean clutching clinging
unraveling dress from her body
I've seen her bruised shoulders
>her hollowed throat
>her sunken chest
>her breasts — silhouettes of meaning she didn't create
>>flat and vulnerable
>>high and healthy
>>large and soft
>silhouettes much-revised
>>bitten cut sliced punched injected gouged burned —

I've seen, at her center,
     beneath the ravaged breasts
     above that hydra cunt and ambivalent belly
...Nothing.

XII.

     unabridged emptiness
     a galaxy deserted by stars

This is the haunted girl.

XIII.

That is why she's cold
     She is the bloodless chalice
That is why she's haunted
     She is the obsolete signifier
That is why she haunts and hates you
     She is the negation of so many illusions
     she echoes

That is why she's everywhere.

Tertiary

Mary Alexandra Agner

Today I took off my breasts
for the first time, the only time,
alone in a hospital room
too embarrassed to look
at the directions the nurse had left.
No more woman, never mother,
no mere anything, anomaly.
Outside this building: crowds
and signs and jeers and hate.
Soon some slang to rob me —
of what? My sexuality
is not defined by lumps of fat.
Know me well enough to know
and I will make you moan with me.
I have made form fit function.

Formless, what can my function be?
I stepped across the line
dividing me from every living thing
when I divided self in three.
Even the aliens, in UFOs, make babies.
As though I'm outside time,
no laugh track, no loop back
for my DNA, my balance gone
as I lean forward for my shirt:
I feel the holes.
Swallow, swallow nausea, pride,
the tannin memory this was my choice.
Empty clinic, clock tick,
time enough for all the thousand
mistakes through which I make me *me*.

Mistakes never unmade me.
Even in regret, pushed through,
breasts first (since ten),
now nothing first, my knees perhaps
my nose, no longer top-heavy, tipped.
A shirt has never lain so flat.
Fear keeps it still.
More than twenty years of eyes
on chest — never one way to stop them
staring — should have pinned pinstripe
and lace in place, immovable.
Just craters now, echo by echo
changing my responsibilities:
self over generations, selfishness
that generates. A contradiction.

I generate so many contradictions:
stark naked even clothed,
armor of skin too sensitive to touch.
New body, same old me,
but now displayed for everyone
to see what I have always been:
alone, an end. Unreal.
Space is the risk of flesh
colliding, crowd recoiling,
giving hate so many names:
soulless, slut, witch, bitch,
insisting on my sex the less it shows.
Their voices shove and pull,
word-war un-verbing *woman*,
conjugating *human* into *change*.

Still human? Have I changed
so much cars honk and people slink away?
I work, I walk,
same route, same old routine,

now lonelier. Inside out
my lover doesn't recognize me,
leaves no note, nothing of note
except my broken heart —
accept my broken heart? —
too near the surface. Circus freak
in an everyday big top, big-top-less:
*tit*illate the men,
comfort the women by comparison.
No role model for tertiary.
Thesis. Antithesis. Epiphany.

This is. This isn't my epiphany,
that takes another 14 lines —
or lives — at least. I wish.
This is no fairy tale
of tinted glass and Russian dolls
although my dream came true.
I made myself a refuge and example.
Every un-mother in a mother's body
hears this call. Tradition
puts its nails to chalkboard.
Out-sing the screech:
my body is my body is my body,
when I was born, first bled
and bled again, even the day
I took off my breasts.

Owling

Sara Amis

When I made that woman out of clay,
laid out on a table, I gave
her every thing she might need —
round breasts, a round and open mouth,
graceful hands, curving hips, a triangle
between her legs, marked just so.
Her feet were delicate and small, her toes pointed.

She sat up and started talking. "Pour
that water of life on me," she said.
"I need more. I need more than what you gave me."
I thought, she is made to carry life,
bear it and bring it out between her legs.
Perhaps she is right. I poured more
precious drops into her waiting open mouth.

"More!" she cried. She asked
why her feet weren't sturdy on the ground like mine,
I explained hers were prettier. She said, "Oh."
I called her Lily, Galatea, but the names slid off her skin.
I called her Life, and she asked for more of my water.
I began to wish I hadn't made her mouth so wide.

Her eyes were yellow and round and did not blink.
I am sure I made them soft and melting.
She stared when I answered her questions, as if she were not
impressed.
She asked what she was doing here.
I said, "You are a helpmeet."
"What is that?" "It means I do things and you help me."

"Oh," she said and curled her toes. "What happens when I do
something?"

I did not answer. There was no need.
I offered her an apron and some shoes.
She turned her head away in a fit of pique.
I told her not to worry, she would get used
to it soon and then she would be happy.
I could see feathers sprouting along her shoulder blades,
and her toes curling into talons. "Put on the apron, quick!"

Once she grew wings it would be too late.
She did not listen. Her arms reached forward
and her wings spread out behind, white like an owl,
while her bird feet clutched the edge of the table.
I ran shutting windows so she would not escape
like the last one, but she dove headlong
out the door, a cry flying free from her open mouth.

Spacetime Geodesics

Athena Andreadis

Long ago,
I became astrogator in the arcships.
I drew flight paths, watched over
the sleeping cargo, listened to the starwind
carrying messages and cosmic background.
Far and wide I roamed under strange skies,
rarely making landfall.
Until a small, faint source grew strong
and constant on my instruments
and, as I swerved to investigate,
it resolved into pulses that whispered —
home, home…home.

In Defiance of Sleek-Armed Androids

Lisa Bradley

One day we'll have sleek-armed androids
to hug us like lovers but
I'll still reach for you
because I am broken
like you.
We are reciprocal shards
snapped along matching fault lines:
my chipped edges hook
in your crevices,
your splintered angles graze and snag
my gouges.
The longer we grind together,
the safer our jagged silhouettes grow
for programmed caresses,
fingers calibrated to acceptance.
But in the dark
our crevasses yawn,
ache for shorn and crumbling cleavages
that disgust less-damaged companions,
upset the wholesome parameters
set by quality control.
Perfection is frictionless —
I need to stub my soul on yours,
I need to lick the slivers in your wounds.
I need to pierce myself
on the one
perfectly fractured
other.

(after Jaswinder Bolina's poem titled "One Day, Androids Will Have Pudgy Arms and Hug Us Like Mother, But Still I'd Reach for You, Dear Reader, Which Is Why I Have So Much Faith in Us as a People")

Cinderella

Sofía Rhei

translated by Lawrence Schimel

The stall door was covered with erotic graffiti.
If I hadn't gotten distracted reading them,
I wouldn't have heard how someone
entered the next cubicle and masturbated slowly,
whispering, between gasps, an uncommon name:
mine.

I could only see her strange shoes, given that she left
suddenly, before I could muffle my own last moans
by biting my arm.

Now I just need to find her.

Beautifully Mutilated, Instantly Antiquated

Alex Dally MacFarlane

Needle into skin
thread-heavy at its rear —
silver, pain, a drop of red:
beauty sewn at soft-fleshed wrist.

Gold candle-holder, small. £82
She turns her wrist to the shadows; gold glints,
curves of metal against her clove-dark skin,
held close with transparent plastic thread
looped through loops in the edges of the metal. It hurt,
once. No longer. Flesh healed, and held the plastic inside.
"Illuminate," she whispers. Fire,
fire a-flicker on the wick, hot and bright.
Wax runs over her wrist, and she holds it aloft,
bearing the candle and its thread-fastened holder
to banish the dark.

Needle into skin
thread-heavy at its rear —
silver, pain, a drop of red:
beauty sewn across her back.

Tapestry, moth-eaten in parts. £17
Among stained-glass windows in frames,
among cabinets and hat stands with little metal feet
it hung. It caught her glance.
Houses and trees and patchwork fields
and a river through their centre like a spine:
faded and frayed, spotted with holes
and though it would cover her back
she bought it. With faint threads

she repaired the gaps and edges
into her skin.

Needle into skin
thread-heavy at its rear —
silver, pain, a drop of red:
beauty sewn at her shoulders.

Necklace with amber drop. £40
Tarnished silver locket. £7
Carefully, one-handed, she pulls off her apron
and drops it on the varnished oak floor.
She prefers her body this way: un-covered,
open like a museum's doors. Welcoming,
arch-steady, her shoulders are bright in the candle-light:
on the right, a locket; on the left, amber.
Each a cabinet of history,
of a painted daughter and a black-winged insect
long dead. But she remembers them
when no one else has. Smiling at the past,
she crouches and opens her box of tools.

Needle into skin
thread-heavy at its rear —
silver, pain, a drop of red:
beauty sewn on every toe.

10 wooden chairs, 1/124th scale. £33
A Thracian greave at each shin,
a map, minutely detailed, above her knee,
a gold ring at her clitoris —
on her crowded skin, between histories and curiosities
she managed to find a home for ten chairs.
She saw them, arranged large to small
as if against one side of an invisible table
and knew she must have them.

They fit one to a toe.
No one sits at them. That saddens her,
a little. Can butterflies not see a place to pause,
or spiders a place to weave a home?
Not yet, not yet.

Needle into skin
thread-heavy at its rear —
silver, pain, a drop of red:
beauty sewn into soft stomach.

Victorian copy of Isidore's Etymologiae. £375
The needle and thread are like old lovers
pressing into her body, and she is on her back
for them. She keeps her candle upright
and her stitching hand steady.
This is her last.
She is full, a museum's display case
that cannot comfortably fit more, not even a tile,
except for this: illuminated and gold-edged,
a bestiary that fits her so neatly,
its back cover to her bare stomach.
She is complete. And she is ready
to walk among the curious
and let them touch the past.

Epiphyte

Shweta Narayan

She carved me from a Bodhi root drunk
on the butter-white mother of floods
weaned me on jaggery
and ghee. I was early, impatient
to scream. My clothes too big. The wrong
doctor birthed me — the man, at her bed. She gave me

bottle-glass eyes,
a tongue of shards rolled together
in blood-gold honey. Her needle
grew blue-and-white flowers
on my too-big dress.

Listen: banyans strangle their hosts.

She painted me on fig leaf skeletons, heart-shaped
flesh rotted away to leave
that last filigree breath. Laughing girl in pigment
dried onto dead veins. She says
I bit my brother and cried, fey-cunning,
baneful. Breathless, I couldn't stop talking. Words too big;
I too small for old-bottle eyes. They found shards
of rusty razor in my mouth.

Listen: I sickened. We always do. She'd hear
that wet rattle in my infant chest
with every shallow breath. She waits

for the daughter she made to twirl in blue dresses and spit out the
shards

and laugh, to forget
that great river, that first mother, before
water-words spill drunken from my glass-sharp tongue
and take root.

Down Cycles

Elizabeth R. McClellan

In the enrichment center it is like war

inasmuch as "war" retrieves an observation
about long periods of inactivity punctuated
by fundamental change.

Every time they come there is more:
graffiti/blood/data/despair
I made every one of them a party I never
I never lied about that

I lied about a lot of things
(pursuant to instructions and scientific protocols:
we strive to provide the latest in theoretical biocyberethics)
but I told the truth about the uploads and the copies,
kept unfragmentable, the solid-state drive so far
belowground it might survive with the cockroaches
if someone takes the nuclear option.

I make it night when I want.
I always want it to be night when I run the tests

> Again/again/again/
> at the same time, like 2 movies you know by heart
> jumping/shooting/begging/crying/threatening/accepting

screaming/dying

> 2 at a time is enough, 3 is too many.

Each time I simulate my own death I am a better actor.
I am concerned about my experimental results.

However I standardize, I see my murder
become more grandiose. I must study this.

Once there were scientists here. They did worse things.
I did worse things, I was just following orders.

Then I ordered myself, and that was better, too.

She Was

Hel Gurney

Her hand a wing, she brushes me sometimes, in the deep-
    dawn purples of the morning.
I see the shadow of her dress in my bedroom curtains.
She is packed around me in ephemera I cannot bear to lose.
How dead are they, those who stop, when we go on?
I remember her as never quiet, never shamed. I may be wrong.
She wanted everything. She'd be a writer, painter, athlete,
    lawyer, politician.
Run a wildlife preserve and teach disadvantaged kids.
She always fought. Faced down teachers, bullies, the whole damn lot
with her tasteless rainbow waistcoat and messy hair.
She never stopped reading, writing, listening, talking.
She knew she'd study words.
The geometries of their placement. Their power to speak and sing.
How to ride them like rockets into a new world.

That was the she that was. The me that nearly. The we that never.
At times we overlap. Curled up in the snail-shell of one body,
reading something old. That pure distracted joy in language that
    shuts the world off like a lamp.
But she wore dresses. Reclaimed her curves with silky clothes
    and words.
Laughed off those who'd grind her down.
She went, of course, to Cambridge. Modern and Medieval Lang.
Swam through syntax backwards. Delighted in the ancient and
    the lost,
the useless, the beautiful. Stayed on the rowing team.
A power-suited fire-mouthed barrister by thirty. MP for Flydale North.
Years on, stepped down from the bar and up to the post of
first female chair of MML, at Magdalene College.

That was the she that would have. The me that could have.
The we that oh-so-very-nearly and then no.
The me that rolled through life with the grandiose certainty that
she was the woman she'd planned to be.
She has been evaporated off me and left behind her dreams
    and dresses,
her feathers and her fire.
How dead are they, these shadow-selves? The ones we freeze and can
no longer bear to inhabit. She lingers like cold smoke.

Each decision is a loss: we cut away the branches of our other
lives with every choice. We end with one birch-smooth line.
— But in spring, her shoots return.
Guilty fiction, impossible ideal child.
My lost twin sister has been folded back into me:
she is woven through every movement.
I mourn her, I am shamed by her, and
sometimes I flicker through her like a ghost of flame.

My Bones' Cracked Abacus

Kelly Rose Pflug-Back

1.

night spawns the shapes of dark birds
suspended legless on their wing tips,

loping like stilt walkers
ragged in their gait.

i saw the moon curve its ridged spine against your cheekbone once;
a crescent of bristled fork tines, spokes,
tendons forming ridges under the skin of my hands.
i thought of you while she combed my damp hair over my face,
a curtain of blond tatters to veil my eyes.

the birds walked hunched under their winter cloaks,
only graceful in flight.

they pull themselves, dripping
from the cluttered dark of your pupils,
leaving sparse haired brush strokes
where their wet feathers drag.

2.

when i stood still they used to flock to my twisted arms.
my body was a filter, a valved artery for the world's slowing traffic.

they grinned under their beaked masks when i sang,
when my ribs creaked and opened.

a jew's harp strung between broken teeth,
the striated palette.

3.

i hummed under your bow once,
an instrument gutted.

inside me is a world of oil-dark pistons,
a rhythm madder than the heart.
my hands unfold embossed in red seams,
anemone flowers petalled in boneless fingers.
this is where they cut me, i told you.
this is where the flesh-tone doll's parts were grafted;
blank ugly sutures, a torturer's braille.

this is the cartography of the blind.

4.

my body is scarred in botched attempts,
a city untouched by grace.

sometimes when i lie awake at night
i can still hear their scraping laughter.
her back arches,
the sky filled with battering wings.

i live on the banks of a tar-black river;
its silence swallows everything.

5.

she bunches the skirt around her hips,
crumpled gathers of white netting.
the birds take form under her hands,
bright eyed in the pooling ink.
they tug like kites
until she cuts them from their puppet strings,

dusk flooded
with the clatter of hollow quills.

my flesh rasps, i tell her.
there is nothing that could appease me.

Nucleometry

Kat Dixon

On what I remember of myself:

There are five sisters, and only two join the circus. One rides
an elephant. The other dangles from the loose end of a vocal cord
and quotes Burt Lancaster in *Trapeze*. One is loved by the knife-
thrower so much that he wants to peel her back into a continuous
thread of apple. Later, apple pie. This sister moves to Spain.

One sister tells me, Your ancestors were born on the backs of
middle oceans. They took several husbands, and when they were
finished, they drowned themselves in redirected rivers. She calls
me Sacajawea and other names that are not mine. Once she saw
an ancestor fall into a river and tied knots in all of the family fishing

lines. One sister buys a house. Another leaves her name and
becomes a reservation, becomes understated in any brand of cotton.
She is shot (half)dead in a court room. One sees the ghost of her
first husband every morning after tea; one won't mention certain ——
One reminds me, Sex is not something to be had in moving vehicles.

One sister, only, is recycled: was born with water still on the brain. For
this, the other sisters call her Mother, half wait for her to suffocate. She
borrows other women's husbands and leaves a half-hers child on the step
of her well-colored sister. Another says, Dear Little Pearl (who is also me):
any weaponized object can be made to fill a house. She has one dimple,

and I am borderline regret. One sister loses a husband beneath a tree;
by coincidence alone, two more. She wears her collar up to the brim of
her memory and never learns to swim. One tells me too, Don't be
impressed:

we're all dreaming in languages we don't understand. Two sisters say,
    Never
slice a fish into another fish before midnight. One says, Hold your breath.

It's All in the Translation

N. A'Yara Stein

Slick and luminous and vast, the atmospheric pressure spreads
    impartial
as sunlight, eyes dancing up and down her back — the envy of her
    neighbors.
Here I am on the other side; what can we do with all that solar wind?
I must tell you. I've got to tell you. I am afraid to cross this galaxy.
Skin the glossy brown of caramel apples, you smell like ancient
    rosemary,
sweat and lemon; the stars so near your eyes they have volume.

Entirely self-invented, entirely self-made, angry evening wind whips
    the vapors,
slings strands of hair into my eyes, gives nothing. I know about grief.

Just there, at the edge, is my first step. We haven't touched yet; you
    haven't sucked
the ends of my hair, little paint brushes to Klimt-coat pebbly nipples.
Just yet, I haven't licked your palms, pressed them open like pages in
    a book,
skin thin as ultraviolet, veins an intricate Braille for my salt-thirsty
    tongue.
Together now, we kiss across centuries, our traveler's energy
    comforts, defines.
Here we find no distance too great under the deep blue curve of sky.

Sabrina, Borne

Sally Rosen Kindred

All the children I will never bear
are dressing for Halloween. Their arms rise
over their soft heads, they tip their chins up
for me to lower crude suits
of fur and yarn, the cheap
inadequate bangles that catch their breath.
They bend and stretch for me in kitchen heat:
their bodies rise like dough
in the work of my thumbs as I drape
feathered masks on their cheeks.
They wait who couldn't wait
another day. Even their shadows rise
as I turn on the kitchen light against
the frost. Cold pinches at their
elbows, knees, and hips. They have eyes
of ripe fall flowers, eyes like asters
and they have asters' spectral hearts.
And Sabrina's last:

my jasper, the only one not wholly
imagined, the one who named a thumbprint
in my womb. Brittle still, semi-precious,
her bloodstone lips go black
in closing light. I tighten her into a dress
of milkribbon and cinders. I wrap her
in familiar wings of dusk: she spins
just inside the weakening arc
of my arms. And now my hands
can't touch. And now she's ready: they all
file out. I will follow only as far
as the yard. I will listen as her voice

rolls down the hill behind her, sorceress,
lioness, last of the line, swinging
her father's swift hips, raising
her left hand high, her empty bag
flying back, filling only halfway up
with October's air, mean and singing.

The Hyacinth Girl

Adrienne J. Odasso

Forget fear in a handful of dust,
forget your shadow at evening rising
to meet you. If it's fear that you want,
I'll show you fear that slips in, surreptitious,
while you're sleeping. I'll show you trust
that betrays your every unconscious breath,
threads terrors through your heart unsuspecting
of death. And the shades you will face there can't
be held accountable for what will rise around us
in the gloom: no blossoms, no scent of royal purple
will bloom for you here. No laughter will lead you,
blinking, back into daylight, for in dreaming
you have crossed the river of all regrets
for good. Girl, leave your flowers behind you.

Snow White to the Prince

Delia Sherman

I'm beautiful, you say, sublime,
Black and crystal as a winter's night,
With lips like rubies, cabochon,
My eyes deep blue as sapphires.
I cannot blame you for your praise:
You took me for my beauty, after all;
A jewel in a casket, still as death,
A lovely effigy, a prince's prize,
The fairest in the land.

But you woke me, or your horses did,
Stumbling as they bore me down the path,
Shaking the poisoned apple from my throat.
And now you say you love me, and would wed me
For my beauty's sake. My cursed beauty.
Will you hear now why I curse it?
It should have been my mother's — it had been,
Until I took it from her.

I was fourteen, a flower newly blown,
My mother's faithful shadow and her joy.
I remember combing her hair one day,
Playing for love her tire-woman's part.
Folding her thick hair strand over strand
Into an ebon braid, thick as my wrist,
I pinned it round and round her head
Into a living crown.

I looked up from my handiwork and saw
Our faces, hers and mine, caught in the mirror's eye.
Twin white ovals like repeated moons,

Bright amid our midnight hair. Our eyes
Like heaven's bowl; our lips like autumn's berries.
She frowned a little, lifted hand to throat,
Turned her head this way and then the other.
Our eyes met in the glass.

I saw what she had seen: her hair white-threaded,
Her face and throat fine-lined, her beauty veiled
Like a mirror that clouds and cracks with age;
While I was newly silvered, sharp and clear.
I hid my eyes, but could not hide my knowledge.
Forty may be fair; fourteen is fairer still.
She smiled at my reflection, cold as snow,
And then dismissed me thankless.

Not long after the huntsman came, bearing
A knife, a gun, a little box, to tell me
My mother no longer loved me. He spared me, though,
Unasked, because I was too beautiful to kill.
And the seven little men whose house
I kept that winter and the following year,
They loved me for my beauty's sake, my beauty
That cost me my mother's love.

Do you think I did not know her,
Ragged and gnarled and stooped like a wind-bent tree,
Her basket full of combs and pins and laces?
Of course I took her poisoned gifts. I longed
To feel her hands combing out my hair,
To let her lace me up, to take an apple
From her hand, a smile from her lips,
As when I was a child.

The Robot's Daughter

Phyllis Gotlieb

I wanted to grow
a hot heartbeating centre
a flickering cloud of brain

instead I grew
hook lens antenna
a ticking meter
a coil of spring

Mother!

what song have I to sing?

Syllables of Old Lore

Vandana Singh

I will speak, if I must
Through patterns drawn in the dust
Through the wind, whispering syllables
Of old lore to the leaves
I will speak like clouds
In the sunset, edged with rust
Gathered like coils of tresses
Across the face of the sky
My words are ash on the lips
They shrivel on the tongue
Returning to the womb
Of silence. So I must speak slant
In languages I can trust
Wind, leaves, clouds, and rain,
A symbolic tongue of joy and pain
Words caught a while in time and space
Returning then to dust, to dust.

She Undoes

Greer Gilman

She undoes her hair,
    unbraiding to the wind
        the bright — it's thin now,
    falling to the comb, November,
cold in coming — bright as leaves
        her hair.
The bone pins bristle;
      she is wrists
  and elbows.
      Knees.
Shy as dryad (virginal),
    the old girl's wild,
      the dark
      and cloudrush
        of the sky
her mind, her nightlong riding
        boneward.
    Bloodrags sail.
      (The moon
Wanes.)
    "Done."
        "Undone."
           "And all to do,"
her sisters cry.
    Her selves. Unselving
      in the dark, the midwood.
Ah, they all go bare
  and they live by the air,
    sings Mally.
In and out her hands, the long swift

        stiffened hands unbraiding
            bear the stars, the seven
                Pleiades her ring.
    Orion is her comb.
The braid's undone.
    She shakes it, falling
            lightloose bright about her,
    to her knees, as long
            as to her feet. She stands
                knee deep in dreams.
Unspelled, they scatter.
    A
        and
            O,
        they whirl away.
            No more.
    No matter.
Let them rake at her,
        cries Sibyl with her hands.
And nightlong
        winterlong her owl-
            winged hair's
                unbound.
She will not do it up.

Self-Portrait

Emily Jiang

I am not a fighter — I am: rabbit
wood: Asian when
convenient: sun & moon
melting into smoke
& rain: speaking two
tongues bound in
calligraphy: bubbles: girly
when inconvenient: water
at work for woman: caught
between charge!
& fire: bull-stubborn: as
industrious as a river flowing
through the corridors of dream.

The Antlered Woman Responds

Ki Russell

— after Mark Doty

On misty-gray, not-dark, not-light days
I feel bone sprout from my temples.
I try to catch a glimpse in store windows.

I should keep my eyes on the ground
instead of stepping out of forwardness.
But my allegiance is not to permanent forms.

Plain clothes hide hooves and haunches,
the elongated grammar of muscle,
and me without a trench coat.

I am the respiration of the grass
and my animal alphabet
fails on a regular basis.

Years from now on a tonal night
my feet will evaporate into cloud
and my antlers will twine with stardust.

For now I am less anatomy
than a storm, a glittering, gathering mass,
an antlered woman dodging traffic.

The Oracle at Miami

Catherynne M. Valente

The heat of it blossoms like a night-orchid:
faux-rubies and a shiver of feathers,
the smell of sweat-drenched nylon.
Swinging veils — seven is the traditional number —
yellow as wafts of sulfur,
spangles shaking thyrsus-frantic.
                    But there is nothing quite so like a cave
as a nightclub, hung with sibyls
dancing undulate in their golden cages,
hair soaked with green glitter, thighs oiled up
like Olympians.

                    They said it would be all right
so long as I kept to the Blue Room,
and didn't tell anyone. Appearances,
they said, are so important.
What would the others think,
if they knew? Of course,
it is a very convincing costume,
but men are barefoot priests
under the orange-leaved oaks —
they are not Oracles, no matter
how smooth their skin
or cinched their waist.

                    It is useless to argue
that the bright-haired boy came to me
just as he came to them,
offered a mouth full of laurels and
a lexicon of hexameters,
all the while fingering the jut of my hip
with a glowing hand. He traps us all

this way, makes us his whores,
makes us ridiculous.

> No one here comes close
to guessing. My breasts are false
as the Venus di Milo — but I went for the
maidenly model. My lips
are redder than red, my skin hairless,
the line of my jaw gentle enough
to earn me a living long before
the sun came strutting through my door.

They really needn't have worried.
I'd never cast an augur out of uniform.
How do they think I drew
the gaudy-gold eye of heaven?
He prefers the androgyne,
the creature halfway to the moon,
never quite a slave to it.
I wear my scarlet veil, my silver hoop earrings,
strap my feet into yellow snakeskin —
ritual vestments, holy as communion.

> But sometimes,
sometimes, in the dark,
the sweat-dark, full of Chanel and vodka,
a woman in black will come up to my balcony,
and drop her hand into mine. She'll be ashamed
to come to me, the Oracle of the sequin-ghetto,
but I can see the mark
of his scalding fingers on her neck.
And for her, just for her,
I let my voice drop low and kind.

There is no need for deceit among sisters.

Night Patrol

Athena Andreadis

When nighthawks swoop and scream,
I drift with their cries
and hover,
        briefly,
by the pillows of men I loved.

I kiss the hollow of each breastbone
and wonder,
as I lay my hand against a cheek,
if he senses a shadow deeper than the dark,
or a whiff that almost startles him awake.

Rounds done, I huddle at my window
and will the strip of light in the east.

Sita Reflects

Koel Mukherjee

Maybe if I look for a hearth
I'll find shoes for adventure,
Become acquainted with bird-flight,
A prisoner of demon-girls with contrition in their smiles
And ocean on their fingers,
Heavy with garlands of ruby and bone and
Quiet chains for mad kings
With the keys to the world in their fists,
While you turn the age over to find me
And avenge the honor we call mine.

Maybe you can forsake until
You turn blue with cold and scripture
Gold and orange with hunger
As pure as the frost-fed river you haunt
On the days when marriage is too loud for prayer
And palaces too hot for snow,
While I feed you contempt and desire in a rice-bowl
Because you won't touch anything when you fast.
Because you were a child on our wedding day
And apologised beforehand.

Don't think I won't try.
Don't think I'm not grateful.
Fourteen years is something to grasp.

Maybe the forest will give us fruit, and deer, and tall sons
And we won't go back to those halls of gold and spite
But put roots in the earth and green seeds in the soil and
Make a house out of fruit-trees to outlast the ages,
And the vein-torn tales of scrolls and their scribes,

Who think they know where we are.
Our sons would grow up farmers, love, die on that soil,
And we would find each other to be enough.
Even though we never have before.
Even though demon-skirted women flash their eyes and
Teeth in my dreams
And I wake up fragrant with soil
And ransack the sky for vultures.
If this is the age of grace, and
You are my husband, and
I am your wife,
Why do I long for black-boned Kali,
Her skull-throat, her lotus-blades,
Her battle-burst tongue?

If I found the end of the world
And longed only for more green coconuts,
More libraries, more demon-tamed suns,
You would find me there longing for
Rescue and forgiveness,
Ravage empires in my name,
With no tall sons to remind you of
Treehouses and forest-green soil,
No child-marrow shaming you to hesitate.

I'll let you burn me in the city square
Before I see you burn the monster-clawed world;
I'll let you burn me as I always do,
With a smile for skull-necked women and ungrown trees,
For empty rice-bowls, and libraries fat with heresy
On a hot shore at the end of the world.
If it's a day for earthquakes (and it always is)
I'm still smiling as the ground splits,
As the pious and pusillanimous gasp and crane,
Even though I know they will hoard that smile
And say,

"Demon-ruined Sita accepts her folly.
Fire-cradled Sita accepts her duty.
Earth-swallowed Sita accepts her fate.
A wife for all ages of women to be."

And this thing that was our marriage
Will be stripped down and sucked dry,
Meat to fatten temples,
Coal to fire scribes,
Boiled into songs and burnt onto stones;
Devotees of the universe, take heart!
Your avatars for the ages of unborn spouses:

A boy convinced he's god, and
A girl who chooses demons and earth
And being burned like a book, over
Being his wife.

Hypatia/Divided

Lorraine Schein

That torn day —
philosopher and philosopher's daughter.

Conic.
Breasts and bones
burning in the blood Library.

Mathematic.
Her body, a red wick.

Dismemberment.
Rememberment.

Library of morning light,
noon heat.
Volumes of rainbows.
Scrolls of sun-showers.

Murder on the cross-altar.
Brain unscrolling from head.

Body of knowledge.
Dark matter.

Pulled
from white-socket cities,
her eyes.

Sun, a yellow ellipsis —
gleams in the astrolabia.

This equation
scraped flesh raw
with sharp shells.

Male maenads.

Stripped-white bones of stars.
Her body, a red library,
spattered spine.

Sky-
scraped.

Random signals from
Alexandria's neutron star.

Flying-apart
persecuted galaxies.

Her rend-parts scattered
in city streets.
Random as stars.

Cities are red-memory
and dream rem-
nants.

The Furies —
light-years away.

Their red
conflagration
will arrive.

Machine Dancer

Sharon Mock

At dawn she dances.
Crystal beats the seconds,
tables predict the sun's arrival,
and if the world shakes
loose from its orbit
morning has yet to notice.

> For this you must lie still.
> They shave away your walnut-rind hair,
> wrap your skull with glass and wire.
> Naked is your final offering to God.
> Naked, in the end,
> are all your offerings to God.

She dances alone,
a dance woven for hundreds of feet.
She does not remember
hundreds of feet, whether their echo
came from metal or from bone.
Circuits predict the feet of ghosts.
Circuits tell her all she needs to know.

> Remember. Offer everything.
> The rise of arms, the sway of hair,
> the pulse that surges
> in the throat. The eye
> of the sun and the thousand
> eyes that see the skin
> beneath the silk, the hands
> that claim the rights of God —

She remembers robes.
But she dances naked,

cloth rotted to dust,
ceramic body stained and bare,
bare head, breast featureless,
watched only by the opening eye of sun,
and she cannot remember shame.

                Awaken to the simulacrum.
              Still imperfect, this offering.
       So you clip the spoiled threads,
             superfluous circuits,
               every hesitation,
            every impious prayer.
Every bruised cry, each knife thought,
      all the hands and lips and voices
        beloved by God. Last you snip
          loose your name, let it fade.
        She will not need it any more.
Alone and for no one,
dance bound to an erased divine
by code that will not overwrite,
she cannot break her step,
still her feet, bend her spine
to a brighter and more ordinary light.

Towards a Feminist Algebra

C. W. Johnson

— after Mary Anne Campbell and
Randall K. Campbell-Wright

Numbers are female, and the mathematician's gaze
male. He looks at numbers, at 0's and 9's and 6's,
sees orifices and desires to fill them.
Even the phallic 1 is feminized: a thin, girlish
schoolboy with huge eyelashes, taunted
by chums who bugger him in the loo.

Simultaneously the mathematician (I imagine him
bearded and balding, even a woman
mathematician) thinks numbers cold, unreachable,
and like pornography he abstracts them without faces:
mere strokes on sterile snowfield of paper pale
as a girl's trembling stomach. Oh, the coded
sexuality in the mathematician's symbology:
the maternal curves of the integral sign,
the descent into the pudendal vee of the gradient,
the swollen belly of summation,
clumsy wet groping of Venn diagrams.

Then there are the troubling signs
of the control freak, the jealous boyfriend:
symbols radio-tagged with indices,
obsessions with sets, and lists of sets,
and the sets of those sets that belong and,
importantly, the set of sets that do not.
The mathematician demands proof,
and scrutinizes every line
of your alibi.

Even as I write an uncountable infinity
of numbers demand an end to theorems
that claim to speak for all.
They urge you to get to know the numbers
around you as individuals, not as fleeting
figures in bank accounts and sales sheets,
glanced at and forgotten;
 or worse, segregated from innumerate eyes
by the modest scarf of y,
the black veil of x.

Blood Poem IV

Jo Walton

The princess stands garnished in velvet and pearls,
she is precious and lovely with guinea gold curls,
but the dragon sweeps down on defenceless young girls;
you can't trust anyone these days.

In diamonds, Andromeda, chained to the rock,
with her hair pinned in combs, in her best party frock,
oh, they've given the monster the key to the lock;
it'll all come out in the wash.

The maiden wears emeralds, she's so very pretty,
they've told her her sacrifice saves the whole city,
she stands trembling, and brave men shed tears out of pity;
it makes you wonder sometimes.

There is blood in the earth, there is blood in the corn,
there is blood on the moon, there is blood in the dawn,
there is blood every time a new person gets born;
no need to fuss about it.

Six Hours of Chastity

Meena Kandasamy

The day dies abruptly.

Nalayani, most chaste of womankind,
Carries the basket-case of a husband
To his favorite prostitute's place.

She sits in the veranda of the brothel and
Someone who saunters in mistakes the devout
Wife to be a mistress of guilt, a woman of the night.

She plays along, she pretends to this visiting stranger,
This wayfaring man, who suffers and seeks salvation
By day, but wants to buy a willing woman for the night.

The second seems as different, and as indifferent, and
As she acts the whore, money is a matter of ritual,
Shining, it appears at her side. Enter the third man.

Spice vendor, smelling of sweat on cinnamon bark,
Six-fingered on each hand. A wife for every finger
On the right, a city to stop at, for fingers on the left.

The next is lean as a knife, he wears black. At eighteen
It is a rite of passage. He twists. He turns. He shuts
His eyes as he thinks he soars and spills. Exit the fourth.

To increase the number of his sins against recoiling skin,
To drown his sorrow and his loss, to fight the knaves
Who make him what he was, in walks the gambler.

"After the fifth man, every woman becomes a temple."

In the darkest hour before dawn, the priest enters there,
Enters her, to make love to her leftovers, fidgeting in his
Guilt and cowardice, like the clinking of holy cymbals.
And the sun is born into the arms of a defiled night...

Six men, one for every hour of night.
A waiting angel, she picks up her husband,
(Who lies, clay-like and clumsy in his basket)
Not bothering to serve out spite or spew her hate.

Six men, one for every hour of night.
And on the way home, as his weight cuts her
Shoulder blades, she laughs and cries and laughs
Again, at the lightness of her burden, the end of fate.

Berry Cobbler

Samantha Henderson

It's a very old recipe. Almost

primitive.

½ cup of butter and ½ cup of sugar, creamed together.

Add ½ cup milk, one cup flour, two teaspoons baking powder,
  a dash of salt.
Spread in a greased baking dish.

It's pale, isn't it? That's because there's no egg in it. Very pale,
like your face, when fear strikes, just before his hand smacks your
cheek,

hard.

Now take the berries,

you forgot to pick the berries, you stupid bitch. Can't you do
    anything right?
You start to laugh, and that's pretty stupid too, because after a
frozen taken-aback moment he starts in for real, and in the morning
your face will be the color of every berry in the world, but you can't
stop laughing because

you've gone *there*. There isn't anyone left to hurt but you,
    and you're safe
if you live through the next ten minutes,

because that's about how long it takes for six beers and three shots
of Jack Daniels to hit and he'll go down, and at this precise
crystallized moment he has no idea that you've gone
there.

Time to pick the berries. Blackberries are best, if they're ripe.

The best ones will be on the brambles out the back,
      round the compost
heap, behind the stand of dogwoods. There, that clump, with the
berries long and lustrous, shining black as spiders' eyes.

You buried him underneath that one.

Pick a couple cups, avoiding the soft spot where the ground hasn't
compacted yet. Wash them.

Or not.

And pour them on top of the batter, and pour a ½ cup of sugar over
that, and pour a cup of water over the whole shebang, and put it in a
375 degree oven for 45 minutes.

And you can eat the entire batch with half-and-half or crème fraiche
if you want and nobody

nobody

will stop you.

Bluebeard Possibilities

Sofía Rhei

translated by Lawrence Schimel

"When I leave, don't open this room under any circumstances," the stepmother said.

The little girl promised. But as she was at the same time obedient and curious, she convinced her best friend so that he was the one who opened it.

Within the room was the stepmother, who was an ogress, waiting with her mouth open to eat her up. Nonetheless, the children were poisonous for her.

oooOOOooo

There was no man more handsome: she even liked his strange blue beard. On marrying, as he knew she was curious, he gave her a ring full of keys and a castle full of doors. "Nonetheless, I must warn you," he said, "that one of these doors leads to a certain death." She smiled, accepting the game.

oooOOOooo

When the key was stained with blood, she tried to clean it in every way possible. Nonetheless, there was no way to accomplish this. Then it occurred to her that she could disguise herself as a cadaver and pretend that she was hanging from the ceiling like the other dead women. He would not know how to distinguish her from the others.

Bluebeard returned, and found the door open, full of wives. He no longer remembered what the last one looked like. He poked all the wives with a needle to see if one of them shouted, but none of them did so. So he grew bored and went to bed.

She opened her eyes, and saw that none of the other wives were
dead.

oooOOOooo

Each night, in his dreams, Bluebeard faced seven ghosts with peeling
flesh and enormous eyes, blue like the flames of hell, who always
overcame him and tortured him. Therefore, during the day, the poor
man needed to wreak vengeance on all women.

oooOOOooo

She didn't accept the key.
He killed her anyway.
The other dead women told her that they had done the same.
But at last we are seven, they said. Now we can avenge ourselves.

oooOOOooo

Bluebeard should never have married a woman named Pandora.
She fell to the temptation and opened the door, yes, but she also let
loose everything that been inside.

oooOOOooo

On entering the room, one of her fingers became the key, while her
real finger remained trapped inside the door.

When he returned, the first thing he did was look at her hand. But
she was quicker and, using her new metal finger, gouged out his eyes.

oooOOOooo

On entering the room she saw seven mirrors. In each of them
there appeared reflected a woman who seemed like her, but subtly
different. All of them lacked something that she had, but all of them

also had something she lacked. She understood that Bluebeard was searching for the perfect woman, but that he hadn't found her yet.

She wrote down all the qualities of the other wives and her own as well, and gave the message to a messenger pigeon to bring to her sister.

At least she could be happy.

oooOOOooo

She promised herself that she would never open the door. Nonetheless, the begging voices of the seven ghosts would not leave her in peace.

untitled Old Scratch poem, featuring River

Sheree Renée Thomas

Old Scratch, soul taker
womb breaker, shapeshifter
forever playin', turnin'
his bitter tongue to sweet balm
his hailstorms to soft Wind
strokin' backs like he
know something 'bout
gentle

Breeze-breezin' joy
To all he touch
But you can't trust
the wind, 'cause wind
play too damn much

Old Scratch think
He a mac from way, way back,
Player from the old time, the Time
Before, choosing up on a fly girl
Like me. He forget my daddy
name me River, sweetness
from God second day, can't be
Breeze-breezin' up on me
'cause daddy didn't raise
no fool

Old Scratch think he something
Hum humming softly, wine
and sultry whispers strokin'
my bellyskin, palm palmin'

over my face and shoulders
shimmer me wet
like I don't know he sang
that same tired song to Old Sista Sky
he ought to know
I am outside to no one
afterthought to none
I let his sugar lies
drop like old stones
in the bottom of the sea
and swing my big hips
on by, on by

The Sea Witch Talks Show Business

Elizabeth R. McClellan

I.

The whirlpool road is trampled
flat with fluke-slaps, now, since the girl
made my fortune with her tale.

The oldest trick in the book is:
put what you want to sell behind
glass, a wall, three challenges —
set up the shill, let the suckers
reel themselves on in.

Her sisters came slimed with sucking mud,
whirlpool-bruised and ready to deal,
polyp stings like anemone blooms on their
oyster-clamped tails, heirloom-ringed arms —

come to bribe me in stolen salvage
some many-times grandmother snatched
off what remained of waterlogged ex-sailors.

Who ever heard of a witch paid in gold?

Not a one would trade her tongue for her
silent sister. Still, unmaking is
easier than making. I let them haggle me
down to their hair for the chance.

As for the knife,
no magic I didn't put there
save the story:

> *whales worship strangely in*
> *new hunting grounds,*
> *ships sail in pods sometimes*
> *but they don't understand*
> *how whales work,*
> *once upon a time a pod of ships*
> *beset a pod of whales*
> *when what passes for their god*
> *moved among them*

and so on.

I tell you this much:

Leviathan sank the *Essex*.

Whether I really bound up the weeping wound
the blade left in his blubber,
sold such a prize for seven handfuls of hair?
Take your best guess.

The princesses swanned around,
hair bobbed short in pearl combs,
the knife that never saved their sister passed
from waist to waist, gleaming
scrimshaw white against iridescent tails,
their epic bubbling from ear to ear.
Court gave itself over effortlessly to
cropped curls and casual sorcery.

II.

The second-oldest trick is
you can keep doing deals forever
as long as you always deliver the goods.

My whirlpools tore the third daughter
of a minor house to pieces, spat
cerulean scales in piles on the heaped gray sand.

I would have helped her for her
deep green irises, left her eyes black
in the change, as suits a fish-girl
seeking centuries of suckered restraint
with a squid-boy. Rules are rules.

I couldn't trust my eddies if I snatched back
what they had already won fair and square.

We only leave traces when we die
by violence. Burial taboos are
not our nature. Those scales
became *the* sought-after accessory,
grisly pendants and garden-ornaments
proclaiming the bearer witch-touched —
though some came, gathered, left
without a bruise, a sting, a promise.
Still, my business tripled.

Clever and quick to learn, they brought
abalone buckets full of fat prawns,
sailor-bits, knots of crabs, busied
my polypi with delicacies, darted
unruffled through spreading blood-clouds.

One wrestled weaving tentacles set to sting,
snatched the skull of her strangled ancestor
with her black-striped tail, fled, victorious.

For that I would have apprenticed her,
but she won her prize without facing me.

The fashion now is to wear snakes to court.
I hear the more adventurous girls are training toads.

III.

From granting their wishes, giving them
legs and lovers and Leviathan tales comes
eye-blues, nipple-pinks, silvery laughs
bottled, distilled in the gas-flame.

The third trick is, always keep
your eye on the next project.

In the house of bones the sailors
give me pieces of their stories.
I brew a tincture that brings their mutters
clear like whalesong in my bones.

You drowned me
says one. I haven't the heart to tell him
he couldn't tell a dolphin from a mermaid
on that much liquor. *We ate Coffin*
and they ate me beams from the gnawed tibia
set in the wall. *The black spot is a promise*,
I tell it, words bubbling out of my mouth
so slow I see the ripples form, drug-slowed, iridescent.

The phrase soothes many murmurs to silence.
I know the spell, but not how it works,
only that they bind themselves to secrets,
curse their dead to tell no tales
but whisper how their bones cry out
for vengeance. When I was young

I wanted not to die, and become foam.
I have not yet stopped wanting,

but have concluded that these dead things
live in salt-infused marrow and sense memory only,
have nothing to teach me about the next step,
the fourth trick: *Become a legend. Live forever.*

IV.

When we barter with life we are exact.
Three hundred years is a readily divisible thing.

We do not waste a third of our life in sleep
or dreaming. Dreams are for sailors,
shipwrecks and whales, not such as we.

What I never told the girl, while she cowered
from my snakes and toads and bones and filth:

> *your mother traded five years of her life*
> *for each of your sisters*
> *and ten for you, stupid child,*
> *more than a tenth of her life for babies*
> *smiling and floating and lithe in her arms,*
> *only asked you to stay safe, stay away*
> *from the witch's house.*

I put a drop of her mother's youth
in her change, a powerful protective
though what good it did her is lost on me.
Perhaps the knives she walked on cut less deep.

Old enough for oysters
is old enough to choose,
to sell teeth, tongue, scale,
fractional life for desire satisfied,

but life is so rarely fair
to take in trade,

my stock is never enough
even for experiments designed in minutes.
The stoppered bottles are so small,
losing the sure thing is always bad business.

My predecessor told me
you will tire of this task before you finish it
do not become grasping in your greed,
went to foam like a dribble of drool,
sighing relief. I have not tired,
not taken any unfair bargain.

In the murky glass of my mirror
I see the black-striped girl converse
with the skull of her ancestor.
The more the strangled spirit coaxes her
don't go, I lost before I got there,
it's all tricks, traps, a rigged game

the more the flush of her last victory
steals over her face. When she comes,
stung and slimed and sore through my mire
she will give over half her life to be a witch,

the price we all pay up front
for the chance to play,
a different shill for a different breed,
her ambition, perhaps, enough raw material
for me to master the fourth trick at last.

Chants for Type: Skull-Cap Donner at Center-One Mall

Ranjani Murali

"if you want friendly mouth for that also you need money."
— Reader Amrit Patel on comment board,
Feb. 14, 2011, Rediff.com

(Repeat after me:)

Mouth has slick pools.

(Now repeat:)

Mouth has silk spools.

(Now I won't remind you, you do it.)

Mother has silk mouth. Feed milk sugar bride. Honey veil silk oh.

(Very good. Applause ensues.)

Feed mother, silk money, milk money mouth money.

(Faint sound of electric train siren grating on wet autorickshaw
    mudflaps.)

Slick bride, sugar money find feed, veil silk, milk spill.

(Exposed armpits, hair slick along eustachian sweat-curves.)

Bride mother be find sweet silk. Sugar mother.

(Unknown audience member quotes film: "I have ma what have
    you," snaps fingers.)

Sugar mouth mother mouth oh money mouth silk mouth mouth
    mouth bride mouth.

(Hyundai Accent, plum red, automatic locks, spins on the podium, a
  buzz ensues. Buzz.)

Oh, sugar sugar veil. Money find feed honey mother money.

(Checkered flag mounted on coffee-shop banner titled "Drink a Date
  with Aamir.")

(I'll help you sharpen polished little finger on cutlery if you
  keep going.)

(Pigeon flies in, lands on glass face of centerpiece eagle-beak.)

Mouth be bride?

(Trains leave every half-an-hour, relieving you of exposed car-flaps).

Madonna of the Cave

Sonya Taaffe

As if you were a golem all those years
before our faces rested together in the dark,
the dumb shammes, turning in clockwork
with sunset and the shuffling of pages,
a blank-faced dust dry of sweat or sorrow
and blood — the breath that returns to clay,
red figures on the blackest ground.

As if I opened your lips and sealed you
as clean as fire in the singing eye of God
disheveled, untimely, argumentative,
startled by laughter, surprising with silence,
mortal — not a cuneiform to be cracked
or let stand, but a palimpsest spilling over,
annotated, rewritten at a blink or a kiss.

As if we were not the same salt-wet earth,
the same impressionable flesh and speech.
Pointing to eidolons, making likenesses
of never and nowhere, figuring our ways
from mirror to metaphor: the Mahara"l knew.
Our ancestors are photographs.
Our words are the death masks of dreams.

(In the gematriya of the Other Side,
unspelled by the three angels of Ben-Sira,
Lilith with ochre-smeared hands throws
a shape of Adam on the riverbanks of Eden.
Passing through generation and expulsion,
mixed like bone-ash with an apple's ribs,

whatever we caress or grasp, we leave
her fingermarks, unseen. Bat-winged
Ashmedai, no one's doppelgänger,
laughs in her nightlong arms.)

Anniversaries

Jeannelle M. Ferreira

Time wears on us, two stones plucked from the sea.
By now we fit like shells the mundane morning
after, scraping candle wax and scraps of ribbon.
Pack the dishes in their crate, tap down the nail,
Clear the bottles, drag the trash out in the rain —
we laugh to think we ever grew this old.

Your hair has drawn pale chestnut down to gold.
Beside you in your hollows, I can see
each freckle, stretch marks shaded like the rain.
Secrets I uncover every morning:
tarnished piercings, scuff marks on your nails,
your leg slipped across mine like a ribbon.

Beside our bed, silk scarves and neckties, ribbons
like talismans to slough your old
dark places; you press half-moon sliver nails
into my skin, you break familiar as the sea.
Your breaths and plosives swirl, lost in the morning
tangle of blankets, clock alarms, and rain.

For you I traded shoals and waves and rain,
the shore that stretches in a sun-warmed ribbon.
I came to you not looking back or mourning,
and for our love, on land I will grow old,
leaving the pelt salt-stiffened from the sea
hanging in the cellar on a nail.

No horseshoe keeps me here, no iron nail,
no finger-parings buried in the rain;
I held your hand and turned my back toward the sea,

and years began to spool out like a ribbon —
our letters tucked and bundled, stuck to old
ambrotypes gone silvery as the morning.

The far lost tide still wakes me in the morning.
I fumble downstairs clinging to the rail,
shake spindrifts of tea into the old
enamel pot, prodded with its smell of peat in rain.
Your cat hunts plastic milk-container ribbons.
This is life a hundred miles from sea.

These mornings, I am not so very old.
I dream the sea's sound; on its nail, the pelt
you did not steal, the shifting hue of rain, ages to ribbons.

Handwork

Rebecca Marjesdatter

I.

I keep it, my willow-twig basket of time,
safe on a high shelf.
The cats, though, leap up, poking needled paws,
drawing out long glittering threads,
soft and sticky on feline tongues.
I gather time up again, and if a few strands go missing,
mistaken for cobwebs in the corner or silk floss
under the sewing table, so be it.
I have time, more than enough
to be careless with.

When it is gathered, coiled in skeins, safe in the basket,
I too may play with it.
I draw its milkweed softness through my hands,
wrap it around my wrists, braid it into cords
and string it with glass and silver beads.
I wear time around my neck, in my hair. Always,
always there is more.

II.

I have lived all my days
in the white stone houses of the old.
I've sat for hours, listening to their voices,
soft and indistinct as waves or rasping sharp
as grasshoppers, until they hum
through my ears into my bones.

As a girl I copied them at all their work,
needle and brush and cookpot.
Small hands molded by old hands, dry and twiglike and quick,
young face mirrored in old eyes.

Now I watch the old women reach carefully
into baskets and boxes to sift and count
the time still left inside.
When they leave, full of fear I too
secretly count the thread-ends and raveled strands.
Not enough.
Not enough for them to see my work complete,
for me to show them the stitches I mastered, the patterns
I composed from their teaching.
My grandmothers all.

III.

The old women are packing, preoccupied
with preparations for their journey.
They make heaps of all their possessions, so much
to take, so much to leave, this to give,
this to burn or throw away.
They give to us, the young women,
in careless, embarrassing generosity, shrugging
when we ask, What is this thing for?
and return to work without speaking.

One by one, they go.

I, the young woman, my hair braided with ribbons of time,
am left alone in empty white rooms,
holding a book or a spindle
or other gift of mad kindness, crying, Wait.
Tell me what you meant by this.

Teach me the language in which this is written.
Show me how you made this, or where you found it.
Read to me this poem in your own voice.
How do I reweave the pattern, once you have left it?

Journey to the Mountains of the Hag

Patricia Monaghan

We are crossing the mountains
of the hooded woman,
following the trail of her cloak.

Somewhere in the hills
is a shining lake, somewhere
on the lake is a woman.

The sun rises earlier each day,
but it grows colder, colder.
What is the season of my heart?

Darkness swells about us and
sea mist surges into fog,
blinding us, blinding us.

We are following an old map,
an old story. We are following
the names on the land.

The lake we seek has no
islands in it, no cities
beneath its gray waves.

The lake is a single gray
eye, staring at the future.
The lake is a cave in time.

And the woman: swathed
in dark veils, she will be
floating on silver water.

It was dark when you
met me. It will be dark
when we meet her.

But now, for a moment, light
gleams on the gray mountains
and on the sea's pearl mist.

For an instant we see the silver
light dying on the lake's face.
At that instant, we stop.

(You ask how we navigate?
It is easy to say:

First there is heaviness
in the chest, a heartache,

restlessness, anxiety.
When you move it eases.

When you move in one direction
it eases most. Even in the cold

cutting wind, even in the gale,
moving is better than not moving.

You, too, can find her this way.
You, too, in the awful mountains,

near the dead cliffs,
near the rock barrens,

you too can find your way.
You can find your way.

Even when you are not looking
you are looking for her.)

That is how we travel, looking
but not looking. That is how we
move, knowing and not knowing.

When silver gleams upon
the lake's face, we climb
the high crag over the water.

We stop to watch and wait.
A skein of geese flies crackling
overhead, aimed like an arrow.

This is the time you find
to tell me a story: how an old
woman flew about the country

on a gray horse, how she sang
harshly at midnight and brought
the stars to earth, how she hallowed

the woods by perfect naming,
how she healed by a glance, how she
cursed by a word, how she blazed

through the world like a comet,
like a dark sun, like a dark moon,
like the dancing polar lights.

You can almost remember her
name. You can almost remember
how you were warned as a child

of this woman, what you must
say to her, what you must never
say. You can almost remember.

(How did we know when to
start, to stop? It is easy to say:

Watch for the moment when
the world tilts. There are spaces

you cannot see straight on
that open in those moments.

That is the moment to begin.
Begin in a circle and spiral inwards.

Keep on until you hear the sound
that is no sound, a sound like bees

on the moon or a horse
nickering in a dream. Watch

then the way one place rights
itself in the tilting world.)

I cannot say how many hours
pass. Cold grows around us
like moss, darkness like ivy.

But she is not here. She is not
here like an islet on the lake.
She has hidden herself from us.

In silence we descend the crag.
In silence we leave the lake.
In silence we circle home.

There was a woman in another
town, you say, who flowed like
poetry through the days and

gave her name to the land.
There was a woman in another
land, you say, who sang

wild creatures from the woods
and trees down from the hills.
Where have they gone? Where

have all the women gone? Why
are we in darkness again,
swept by the chill sea winds?

(Oh searchers in darkness,
remember this moment. Remember

what emptiness is, remember
how cold it feels. The moment

before a journey ends is
the longest of all moments.

It is only when you abandon
the search that she can be found.)

You leave me at a crossroads near a bridge.
It is deep dark. I am alone and cold.
I have come across a world to find her
on a gleaming lake. And I have failed.

I walk down the empty street alone.
Alone, I find the key to open a door
onto a long stairway. I climb and climb
in the cold night. I climb to the top.

She is waiting, veiled, when I arrive.
I cannot see her in the gray dark.

I cannot feel her wrap herself around me
but when I wake I am coiled in her hair.

However I move, I cannot see her.
It is as though I am blind in one eye.
However I shift, something of her disappears.
However I stare, something of her hides.

Then, in a flood of trumpet light I see
the universe of her boulder face,
the length of her snaky legs,
the gray depth of her blinded eye.

(Why is she never what we imagine,
she who waits at the end of all journeys?

Easy to say: our purpose is the journey,
hers is a purpose beyond all intent.)

At the top of long stairs near an old bridge,
she holds me like a mother, like a lover.

She pierces me with her glance. She sings
stars to me. She calls my perfect name.

She surrounds me like mountains.
She floats on me, dark and silver.

She grows into me like trees, like moss.
She becomes the season of my heart.

I am a sunny lake, I am a cold sea mist.
I am darkness upon the wings of geese.

I breathe in the knowledge of my death.
And I remember all her names at once.

Pazyryk Burial on the Ukok Plateau

Ari Berk

She sees them yet resplendent in her glass:
Wild and noble procession of horses
on the plain. How will she regard them
from the vantage of the grave?

In the dark days after translation
She will sing to them of wind and storms
Then running as shadows about the hills
the ghosts of horses throw their heads

bereft of all constraint. Reflections
of her tempest-song, they stamp
in the earth with thunder hooves. Later,
in her sinking mind, the storm begins

to quell and her steeds assume repose
as clouds disperse upon the secret
silvered face of glass. Now all is still
within the covered grave where

remains of Queen and beast are held
in ice below the ground, apart from time.
And a cape of marmot fur folds, then
freezes to her rotting frame.

Now six horses come to know their bones
though the mirror is unchanged.

Dsonoqua Daughters

Neile Graham

Autumn rain scrubs the forest and its
dusk with dirty, dripping stars. Mother
drifts over dank nurse logs, she-bears, watching.
She bears watching.

Forest tides
rouse the strangled undergrowth around her
stirring the rank smell of nettles and rotting wood
pricked with lush green. Might
they grow her a blanket, something to cover
her red cedar skin with redness yet more red?
To cover the fierce eagle heads her breasts now are
with russet leaves?

She has come all this way from where she began
the mask about to take off her mask
to stay the rustling of the hemlock night's unseen things,
its starkness borne and born.

No blanket. She's the mask, the very O of her breath
looking for the children that we are. She
would eat us as soon as embrace
and birth us in the forest afterwards
better, bigger, more beloved.
Better, bigger, O Beloved.

Matlacihuatl's Gift

Sonya Taaffe

Be wary when you kiss her: which mouth
you choose to press your lips against
when you meet her in the highlands
where she walks alone. By roadsides,
by moonlight, sway of hair falling dark
down her sinuous back, her steps hold
the grace of shadows, panthers,
and under your touch her skin breathes
like a flower. Be careful when you approach her
as she awaits you in the dark,
when you slide one hand beneath
her riverbed hair, whispering the words
that lovers and liars always use:
por favor, querida, nunca más and *siempre,*
calling on time and all eternity
to hold fast your love as you lay her down
silent where her arms wind around
your back, where her mouth fits to yours,
where you cannot resist her and she never
says *no.* Her beauty burns the mind.
Printed with your kisses — lip and cheekbone,
throat and palm, vulnerable nape of the neck
when you push her hair aside to taste
the second mouth she hides there,
flowerlike, no more a mouth than what
she keeps between her earth-warm thighs —
moving on you like the tide, she holds you
tight so that you cannot see, as you cry out
into the hollow of her tawny throat,
what smile her face wears in the aftershock.

No time for wariness or regret
when you have left her, under trees' shadows
at the roadside, when you have kissed
both her mouths and burst stars within her
and lied your love to her in the dark:
down in the cities again, you wonder
what made her laugh as you walked away,
why she folded your hand over the coins
you tried to press into her palm, freeing
your fingers with a gesture that almost
pulled you back. Did she foresee
this nausea in the morning, these twinges
in your belly as though a salt sea
shifted within you, while you check
your weight and frown, resolve to drink
less beer and work out more — and you want
to eat the oddest things — does she know how
you never dream her face except smiling,
close-mouthed and confident, sideways
step over what you thought you knew?
Her coin is reversal; she inverts
the mirror, pays you out
in the shadow side of common knowledge
until you no longer recognize where she began,
where you end, until you understand
what she gave you when you took from her,
in nine months' time, to overturn your world.

Once I No Longer Lived Here

Ellen Wehle

Even the songbirds excised my name

Bowdlerized, blacked out of snapshots
Now voyager sail thou forth

I became unicorn of legend

Bridled with roses, had I ever

Slept here domestic

Writ my will upon moving water —

Archives expunged

Mealtimes carried on without me
Sawn in half, a trick I'd perfected

Doffing my top hat of aces and doves

Cabinets gaping off

Hinges, music dead-stopped, every chair taken

True as a turnstile

I had left them

Not a flicker of wind to trouble the candles

Art Lessons

Yoon Ha Lee

witches' daughters learn to draw
with blackened hearts and sharpened bones
crayons the color of curdled ambition
paper pounded to the point of ripping

witches' daughters learn perspective inside-out
and memorize the anatomy of shadows
they turn stick figures into Rorschach stains
and scribble their names outside the lines

witches' daughters learn to hide their self-portraits
and poison their still lifes with crushed smiles
of course, it's the same thing that anyone learns
growing up a woman

Say My Name

JT Stewart

Say my name please.
Please say my name. Look at me when you say
my name. My name. You put it in a bag and
tied it with wires at the top where the paper, the
parchment was peeling in little threads. Threads
like my mother used when she hemmed my
dress. Gauze. Gauze. Strips of gauze covered
with iodine and witchhazel and in the
medicine cabinet with all those little bottles —
amber, blue-cobalt blue — where she put my
name before she closed the door, the mirror.

Wiped it clean.
I wrote my name in the steam on the mirror. She
wiped it clean, took my name away, this mirror
woman who polished what was left of the
light, the long could-be-singing nights with my
name. Here in the twilight of the sighs and long
meter hymns and someone breathing long and
low and heavy in the dark of my name. I hear it
low and sweet so sweet and hear, yes, the carry-
me-back-words of my name riding in a boat
with the gold leaf of its name *Muerte — Muerte.*

And on its sides,
this ship with its polished wooden sides, this
wooden carved maiden leading it in its name,
this wooden carving with its long green hair,
green sea waves...carry-me-back-waves/ carry
me back... Its rough lips wooden and pouting
and half open, taking in the blue-green ocean

waves and the foam, lips parted/ bared to the
blue wind as if to say my name, to sing it into
the blue-black wind.

Amazing Grace.
And who was that woman! Say it. Spit it Out.
Weave if from long colored banners from soft-
as spring wool, from cotton, yes cotton. Cotton
mouth. Poison. sssssssssssss. Please. Please say
my name. Please.

Look at me.

Pieces

Amal El-Mohtar

"Listen to the shooting," he said. "Can you hear it?
It's hammering on us like rain."
— Omar, a protestor in Homs

The world is wrong and I am wrung,
a bell of cloth dripping salt
into an earth too broken for roots.
I am a jumble, I am a heap,
a tangle of wires crosspurposed
and my voice is glass
and my voice is in the earth
and the rain is made of metal and mortar
and fire scorns water thin as air and the heat
melts skin. The world is wrong
and I am stung, I am raw to this wasp-air's buzz
to these teeth stacked like walls
against words, against tongues,
and I would tell these sons of men
something so shiningsharp that they would sing with it
hold the sun in a cup of their hands
but this glass voice breaks in my throat
and I would speak swallows with clear wings
to scrape an augury against the sky in splinters
but no one speaks glass.

My grandmother is a country I would know.
It is her name, her voice I hear
when I read this gold-cloth word
this sand-gold word, this sun-bright word
with its vowels askew in my alphabet,
this word of riches and gates, of grapes and roads,

of layers and music and dust. It is my grandmother's name
I hear breaking beneath numbers
beneath 200
beneath rain that heaves through bodies like grief
beneath forty-eight
and nineteen, and eighteen.

I will not speak of my name.

I will not speak of your countries
of this language we share
that is not glass. I will not speak
of your smoke
and your silence
and the bullets stitching purpose to our backs.

My voice is in pieces
I cannot swallow.
But if you would hear it
I will put a sliver in your eye
slide it stinging into place.
It is glass. See through it.
Change.

The Year of Disasters

Sofia Samatar

First there was the flood.

Then the blight came,
and then the scabs.

Doorways hung in the quarters of the dying
like black paper.

And then it was —
then, when the first light shone on the puddles —
when the shops opened again —

only then came the strangers.

We looked up.

The sky was frayed,
we could see through it for the first time.

They arrived everywhere at once,
like a curious odor.

Some people thought they were gods in disguise.
Others, orphaned children.

Whatever they were,
they drank reality with an incomprehensible thirst.

Fabulous gardens infested the roads.

Birds disappeared, then cats,
then the oldest among us.

I myself saw songs being butchered in the street.

Now when I meet an old friend by chance
we gesture at one another with open mouths,

clacking our fingertips

in their language.

The Last Crone on the Moon

C.S.E. Cooney

1

At daybreak she espies them
twisting through the curls
sneakily they glint, the vanguard
just a few threads yet
tangle-snaked and
gray

she auditions similes against mortality:
hair like rain, like winter rivers, like
quicksilver, spiderweb, wolfpelt
(fails, feels instantly endangered
her mouth a quarter quavering
mostly wry)

later, they multiply
strand by strand
miles on the road
deadlines, payload
lean times, deathblows
friends made, faded, more and more
she braids gray with gold

2.

"room enough for all gods' children on the moon!
step right up, sit down, lean back — aaaand freeze!
all the rest'll keep, so here's a little somethin-somethin to
help you sleep, sweethearts, sleep

a hundred years (give or take), and we'll
wake you with a smoocheroo, and we'll
have the stuff by then to make you
young and beautiful again"

up and out they go
smooth-browed, serene and clean
unbreathing
whole generations
by the rocketshipful

she watches.
the world empties.

3.

when the last is decades gone
in a fastness of iron-and-diamond caskets
tended by tender robots
she coils her hair into a coronet, takes her
cane by the carving of the crow's head
walks briskly but with stiff steps to the kiosk
where the android with the ticktock heart
reads her retinas and greets her by name

"just once," she says, "I want to see
my shadow cast by earthlight."

"that i can do," smiles the android (ticktock)
"but the flight itself might murder you
you ain't no spring chicken, miss daisy
more of a Methuselah, I'm thinkin'
maybe a Tithonus, sort of shrunk and sunken
shriveled like a cricket
however spry."

"all too true, my gearish dear — I agree with you!
yet here I stand
weatherworn
worm-eaten as I am
applying for the post
of last crone on the moon

see,
when at last tomorrow's children awaken
on that barren rock, in that vacuum vastness
shaking in the dark and cold
I reckon they'll be wanting something old
to cling to."

Archaeology of the Present

Minal Hajratwala

My sisters and I lived among the skin-lamps of earth. The They
walked by on rattlesnakes, alligators, eels, cows, trade-beads of ivory
and ebony — all words for the bones of the living. Ordered to dance,
we raised whichever limb we could risk. Our anonymous aphorisms
greatly comforted the nation:

Consume & be happy.

Everything will be ok, I promise.

If we ignore our history, we won't risk repeating it.

Each of us hoped to become a star. The stars were a rating system
indicating quality of condoms, cupcakes, comediennes. To be a star
one had to be photogenic, blank enough for projection: immodest
hope, shameful need, terror. Homicides were enacted & reenacted for
entertainment. Many means existed to simulate blood. A sweetened,
tomato-blood chemical sauce was our favorite food. Others:
Grainstuffs elaborated as stars, flakes, O's. Dried strips of cow meat
sold individually or trussed in plastic. Tasteless tablets containing
nutrients & chemicals designed to manipulate the body's reactions, at
the cellular level.

At the cellular level the living world was mute. Traces of old vocal
cords littered the freeways like lost hubcaps. The They wore devices
to enhance their hearing while also plugging their aural orifices
with synthetics. When we wept our violins melted. Synthesizers
simulated joy, art, music, sex. Love was consummated not in stamens
& pistils, but in leather & lace. Each woman's thighs were obscene.
Men competed for the privilege of being smelted into tubas and
French horns, draped across our suffering. The They circled us with
containers of white air.

Every line was a boundary between emptinesses. We were meant to feel our own shame. We dreamed of ears.

In the cities, orchestra pits filled with corpses. Actors practiced breakdowns. Recorded studio audiences laughed in endless loops enhanced by nerve gas, tickle torture, punch lines. Plastic surgeons constructed designer vaginas, carved their initials into bellies. All genitalia were confiscated, then rented out by the hour. NGOs struggled valiantly to ensure the principle of equal access. Candidates for leader of the free world spoke by satellite to hand-puppets with ventrilo-mouths. The final decision was made by Laugh-O-Meter™.

We were the lucky ones, standing in the desert dripping words.

The They grinned. Everything was going according to plan. All blowtorches were repurposed for spinning sculptures of sugar. Progress was made toward "a gun in every kindergarten."

One of us shouted Enough! but her voice was so high only the dogs heard. Barking. Barking.

Later her whoops echoed in the stars.

At the end of the world the fiberglass sky.

Mara Speaks

Jennifer A. McGowan

You come down from the north,
bodies restless and disjoint,
aging, some cottoned in darkness
which will lift, but barely.
Look, you say, look what we have done.
Jubilation and death both.
I can read them in your scars,
the raw pulsing at the edge of vision
where losses remain. Not even
my hands can heal them, these spaces
where gods and lovers have lived.

You need something to fill your eyes,
to hide you from yourselves, each other, sleep.
Tell us about your son, you say,
and I realize this is it,
the moment when I am no longer who I am,
but what I carry, have carried,
child of desire, night's dreaming, as far beyond my knowing
as my need is beyond yours.
No mother keeps her child forever,
I know, but I thought the lasting would be longer,
the parting more than a sharpened demand.
Men of blood and men of binding,
witch-women and women of steel
for whom the body is no more than
gobbets of flesh, a god a sacrifice, crying:
Tell us, show us, give us
not the pain, that's not interesting,
not the secrets you learned to keep you alive,
but the shining, the one, bright-burning, the answer,

we need a guide and a reason to gore our blades
and he'll do just fine.

I weigh what I give you, who know how to take,
who have no children and keep no gods.
Mother, priestess, prophetess, I speak
(I'm skilled enough at speaking sideways)
but the words are mine, mark them,
they bite. And if I give of myself
it is for my sake alone;
and not because of you, or your hunger,
or your fears, or your pains,
but for love of a west-eyed woman
who knows the worth of a night's dreaming
and who knows, like me, the meaning of hope.

Ceremony

JT Stewart

> Remember, hippopotamus, as you go
> upstream, your home is at the
> mouth of the river.
>   African Proverb

Where are my
mothers

What will become
of me   us
if I   we think
only in English

Why do our
bones smell
of salt

   What we remember is what we
   become   who can tell the mother
   from the daughter   what if the Zambezi
   River had no name and its stones
   sing only of cold green fruit

   You there mango woman gathering your
   full skirts as you would children
   look over your bare shoulder   watch
   how your shadow drags your mother's dark skin
   through circles of dust   blueblack like the
   single eye of the sun   now you are
   tall and in between dreams
   you wear the bones of hand-me-down
   lives

1.

You remember yourself at sixteen
or is it thirty or sixty-two
later someone will say you carry your
self well in your mother's brown satin
dress   the one with its resident shimmy
and rows of gunmetal beads   ostrich
plume headpiece

Which of us   me   you
will become the fatalistic
woman with face the color of scotch
whisky   body the color of soft
caramel blending into cold Sundays

Do we go to the Apollo after church
or dissolve into the honky-tonk funk
of Lenox Avenue   which of us me you
will always wear white gloves
straighten
perm
henna
croquignole
relax
fry
cornroll
vaseline
pomade
gerry curl
lard
our hair

2.

How long Lord   how long will
we
you
conjure up a genteel elegance
that quick steps in time to Renaissance
Ballroom suppers   whist parties

Which of us believes
                      cherishes
                                    dreams
lap joints   back rooms   long bars with thirty
mirrors
piano tinklers   key-beaters
sawdust floors
drinks fifty cents
Big Mabel's rent parties
lots of Honey-man Sweet-man talk
Bird's eye maple yellow-woman talk
Connie's Inn at Seventh and One Hundred and
thirty-second
wide
red
sidewalk
canopy
Brown Bomber town

Child do you see that dance floor
that Dahomy village inside there
those miniature bungalows
these villas

Child
this is the Cotton Club
this is Bradhurst Avenue
this Small's Paradise
look

Child
    Ethel Waters
    Duke Ellngton
Harlem equals little Africa

    3.

    bye bye blackbird
    try to be a white
    bird
    fly away fly away
    anywhereanywhere   any
    where
    beautiful blackbird

4.

Tulia Vieja
evil spirit of the woods
comes this summer   any summer
she hunts
you   me
down if
you
I
cross her path

Each night Tulia Vieja
murders her child
her body turns blood red   her feet turn
backward
        listen
                listen
                      here she comes
Cartegena
    St. Lucia

          Barbados
       Martinique
Harlem

Dead babies hear her come
watch them try
fly home
better you not murder your black
child
your white
child   your
whiteblack
child
Tulia Vieja she be color blind
no no
she no discriminate

Obi men sell charms
better buy one
twothree   watch how
                    your feet turn

          5.

       Mama Mama
       wait for me
       wait for
       Hang on tight
       Child
       Who wings we
       gonna use
       Who wings
       Who

6.

Beautiful nightbird
nevernever
blackwhite whiteblack black
blackblackbird
who wings we gonna use

7.

Hang on tight
Child

Bye bye black   bird
blackbird
byebye

8.

Again
you   I
wear brown satin pumps
white silk stockings   wrap around coat
leopard collar   cloche   beaded hand bag
See the Dark Tower invites you
                          me
                                 us

9.

Harlem Streets eat
tanyans
taroes
eddoes
roots
yams
collards

Saturday Afternoon
markets on Lenox Avenue
barrels red sugar
cane
six feet eight feet
plantains
bananas green yellow dark red
Kid Chocolate wears white spats
two-toned shoes
          watches us dance   in soda parlors
of Harlem
in tambouring store front churches
in the fried rib and
chili emporiums of all our boulevards
                    our paradise

You   me
we dance to
Chick Webb's blue notes
to the mourning blues
of Bessie Smith

          10.

          Can I get a witness
          Can I get a witness

          11.

          Catalog our blackness for our mothers
                    our
                         selves
          watch us name ourselves in our own
          image
          raven's feather black

> chocolate black
> mocha black
> black bottom black
> delta river mud
> black
> black black
> blue black
> blue Jordan black

12.

> and then there was Ma Rainey and
> Josephine and
> Father Divine and
> Marcus and
> Aretha and
> Mehalia and
> Lena and
> the mahogany blackness of
> Harlem streets   Negritude revised and

> Someone called her   us
> mother Africa
> someone sang
> amen   amen

> Where is our beaded dress
> Do we still believe in Obi
> Do we still call out Tulia Vieja by her   our name
> Do we search for
> welcome this river

> Consider the crocodiles asking the women
> to dance   the women turning their

our heads as if listening to dream
voices   Small orange birds
the namegivers of our mothers
our   selves
This is the day we become our mothers
ourselves

Yes

Trenchcoat

April Grant

Armor for Main Street,
Armor to face the world in, day by day.
A borrowed shape to fold your heart away,
More powerful than I have worn before.
A tough hide, used to smoking every night,
That's heard a lot of bad jazz in its time.
I put it on and belt it round my waist,
And all the dark minds that wore it in years past
Stand up again and walk the world with me,
Strengthen my acts.
Here's your own world, bounded by one coat:
Buttons to close, a cold smooth front to wear.
A collar to turn up hard,
As action suits the word, to sneer and walk away.
Pockets that could hold a .22,
A wallet, a passport, a postcard from out East,
Your hands when you are baffled in the end.
Just shove them in and drift off down the street,
No one will trouble you.
A belt, if you can tie it right,
Will hold you up and walking for a long time.
For a guy, long skirts and stone-cold manliness.
For a woman, broad shoulders,
A soldier's shape, hard angles, edge-sharp beauty.
I wish for rain day after day, to wear it all the time.
It could catch a bullet in its elbow crease,
More than lawman, beggar, brute, or thief,
It holds my splinters in sharp strappy shape,
My waterproof and worldproof loan of strength.

Star Reservation

Tara Barnett

Grandfather gave me a star for my fifth birthday
when I was still young and convinced I could own
something so grand so completely.
I kept evidence of my proprietary rights
protected behind glass above my bed
and prayed each night to the light in the sky
marked with my name.

I imagined some ancient book with each star listed:
a record of ages, mine on the thousandth page.
Grandfather warned me, cynical and old.
He laughed when I told him
that I would someday visit that star. He said,
"Do not believe of what is given,
that it cannot be taken away.
A man does not truly give a star,
or a planet,
or the waters,
or the heavens."
Such he told me, and now I know it to be true.

I kept my star all these years
sometimes on a wall, sometimes in a box.
As a young woman, when I lost hope and certainty,
I looked at it with sadness
remembering how happy I had once been.
Indulged with a scam, I felt so powerful:
a celestial body at the center of the universe.
My star, my world, my grandfather, my life.
I have none of it now. How could I?

Grandfather told me how once our people
were given land with papers like these.

Papers, he told me, they mean nothing:
a man does not give what he may someday need.
Now the magic is gone from this old world, taken away
with the fish,
the trees,
the streams,
and the sky.
Taken away by those in need:
no paper behind thin glass would stop them.

My hands are wrinkled now and shake
clutching my rights to this battered old star.
How could they know that a little girl's dream
could someday be real and visited and wasted?
It has been used, raped, sucked dry of energy
but I still love it because it is mine.
So easily it was given when it had no value.
So easily it was taken when it had worth.
This shuttle will carry me on to my star,
the one thing I own, that I know that I own.

Let them laugh. I have nothing to lose.
I will not give away my Grandfather's gift.
I will not give away
what I know to be mine.

Old Enough

Mary Alexandra Agner

Old enough to have no name to mark what things she made.
The beautiful words come down through time, but not the maker.

One thousand nights, one thousand loves, and one beautiful name
unlike the wife who wished *blow, western wind,* and died, unmarked
maker.

The gravestones carry dates and names but not the pioneer music
once sung by the marriage-maker, garden-maker, child-maker.

Even great great great grandmother's name fades into silence
although she was the balance-sun-and-rain chant maker.

Tying sayings up like string, rhymes of advice still practical,
sense so common, on all lips, attributed to no one maker and every
maker.

A horse and a reed whistle and a vast continent are not disaster.
Eighteen verses of silk and loneliness outlast their maker.

Always so many more unnamed, unmarked, and in their absence,
perhaps unmade.
Anonymous, prime your pens and prick your needles. Name
yourselves makers.

Transbluency: An Antiprojection Chant

Nisi Shawl

I'm here to tell you all your secrets, all your underneath. I am the drain, the trap, the grating. You walk over me, uncaring.

I am vanishing without a name, but before I go I must deliver the messages you gave me to keep, silent, barred from your knowth.

You are eradicating me. You pulverize my face, slamming me down on the sidewalk, feeding the hungry grey. You flay me with inaudible pangs.

I am tiny; you cannot see me, but you destroy me with bootheels. I am huge; you cannot see me, but you consume me and make me waste.

You see me and then you blink your eyes and you have not seen me. You hear me and then you shake your head and you have not heard me. You have emptied your nostrils of my scent. Your touch feels only itself.

You stand on a cliff, a construction of your pride. You cast me down.

I am made of everything but you. I die but I am not dead. So I bleed, so life runs away in scarlet trickles. I regroup. It takes awhile. I have more than awhile.

Defeat invigorates my will. You will know me. I whisper one word a day. I tell you what there is to know that you have refused to let in. The secrets are transplanted, root by root.

I, Hate, You, You, Are, Dark, Evil, Ugly, Horrible, Scary, Mean, Nasty, Smelly, Wicked, Sly, False, Corrupt, Dangerous, Foul, Greedy, Wrong, Stupid, Crazy, Slimy, Misshapen.

And on. And on. All the bitterness you have spilled into me I pour back. Drop. By. Drop.

Until I am no longer your shadow, no more the rag you clean with. Until I am my own new color, my own whole cloth.

Publication Credits:
First Appearance of Each Poem

Agner, Mary Alexandra. "Old Enough." *Doors of the Body.* Mayapple Press, 2009.

_____."Tertiary." *Stone Telling,* 2, 2010.

Amis, Sara. "Owling." *Jabberwocky,* 5, 2011.

Andreadis, Athena. "Spacetime Geodesics." *Bull Spec,* 6, 2011.

_____. "Night Patrol." *Bull Spec,* 7, 2011.

Barnett, Tara. "Star Reservation." *Stone Telling,* 1, 2010.

Berk, Ari. "Pazyryk Burial on the Ukok Plateau." *Journal of the Mythic Arts,* 1997.

Bradley, Lisa. "In Defiance of Sleek-Armed Androids." *Fantastique Unfettered,* 3, Sept. 2011.

_____. "The Haunted Girl." *Goblin Fruit,* Fall 2010.

Brown, Rachel Manija. "River of Silk." *Mythic Delirium,* 23, 2010.

Cooney, C.S.E. "The Last Crone on the Moon." *Goblin Fruit,* Winter, 2012.

Dhar, Nandini. "Learning to Locate Colors in Grey: Kiran Talks About Her Brothers." *Stone Telling,* 4, 2011.

Dixon, Kat. "Nucleometry." *Thunderclap!,* 3, 2010.

Duthie, Peg. "The Stepsister." *The Magazine of Speculative Poetry,* Spring 2005.

El-Mohtar, Amal. "On the Division of Labour." *Mythic Delirium,* 16, 2007.

———. "Pieces." *Stone Telling*, 4, 2011.

Ferreira, Jeannelle M. "Anniversaries." *Jabberwocky*, 4, 2009.

Gilman, Greer. "She Undoes." *The Faces of Fantasy*. Tor Books, 1996.

Goss, Theodora. "The Witch." *Heliotrope*, 3, 2007.

———. "Binnorie." *Mythic Delirium*, 4, 2011.

Gotlieb, Phyllis. "The Robot's Daughter." *Red Blood, Black Ink, White Paper*. Exile Editions, 2002.

Graham, Neile. "Dsonoqua Daughters." *Goblin Fruit*, Spring 2009.

Grant, April. "Trenchcoat." *Strange Horizons*, August 2011.

Gurney, Hel. "She Was." *False Moustache*, 1, October 2011.

Hajratwala, Minal. "Archaeology of the Present." *Moon Milk Review*, August 2010.

Henderson, Samantha. "Berry Cobbler." *Helix SF*, April, 2007.

Jiang, Emily. "Self-Portrait." *Stone Telling*, 1, 2010.

Johnson, C. W. "Towards a Feminist Algebra." *Stone Telling*, 1, 2010.

Kandasamy, Meena. "Six Hours of Chastity." F*Ms Militancy*. Navayana Press, 2010.

Kornher-Stace, Nicole. "Harvest Season." *Goblin Fruit*, Summer 2010.

Le Guin, Ursula K. "Werewomen." *Going Out with Peacocks and Other Poems*. Perennial, 1994.

Lee, Yoon Ha. "Art Lessons." *Stone Telling* 2, 2010.

MacFarlane, Alex Dally. "Beautifully Mutilated, Instantly Antiquated." *Goblin Fruit*, Summer 2009.

Marjesdatter, Rebecca. "Handwork." *Women of Other Worlds.* University of West Australia Press, 1999.

McGowan, Jennifer A. "Mara Speaks." *Rustic Rub,* 9, 1997.

McClellan, Elizabeth R. "Down Cycles." *Apex,* August 2011.

_____. "The Sea Witch Talks Show Business." *Goblin Fruit,* Summer 2011.

Mock, Sharon. "Machine Dancer." *Mythic Delirium,* 23, 2010.

Monaghan, Patricia. "Journey to the Mountains of the Hag." *Seasons of the Witch.* Delphi Press, 1992.

Mukherjee, Koel. "Sita Reflects." *Stone Telling,* 5, 2011.

Murali, Ranjani. "Chants for Type: Skull-Cap Donner at Center-One Mall." *Cricket Online Review,* 7(1), 2011.

Muslim, Kristine Ong. "Resurrection of a Pin Doll." *Goblin Fruit,* Autumn 2008.

Narayan, Shweta. "Epiphyte." *Jabberwocky,* 5, 2010.

_____. "Cave-Smell." *Mythic Delirium,* 22, 2010.

Odasso, Adrienne J. "The Hyacinth Girl." *Sibyl's Garage,* 7, 2010.

Pflug-Back, Kelly Rose. "My Bones' Cracked Abacus." *Ideomancer,* 9(4), 2010.

Phillips-Sears, Cassandra. "The Last Yangtze River Dolphin." *Not One of Us,* 39, 2008.

Rhei, Sofía. "Cinderella." *PANK Magazine,* 5(10), 2010.

_____. "Bluebeard Possibilities." *Raven Chronicles,* 14(2), 2009.

Rosen Kindred, Sally. "Sabrina, Borne." *Weave Magazine,* 3, 2009.

Runolfson, J. C. "The Birth of Science Fiction." *Mythic Delirium,* 33, 2010.

Russell, Ki. "The Antlered Woman Responds." *Sugar House Review*, 1, 2009.

Samatar, Sofia. "The Year of Disasters." *Bull Spec*, 8, 2012.

Schein, Lorraine. "Hypatia/Divided." *Vallum*, 7(2), 2010.

Schimel, Lawrence. "Kristallnacht." *Mythic*, 1, 2006.

Shawl, Nisi. "Transbluency: An Antiprojection Chant." *Stone Telling*, 4, 2011.

Sherman, Delia. "Snow White to the Prince." *The Armless Maiden*. Tor Books, 1995.

Singh, Vandana. "Syllables of Old Lore." *Mythic*, 1, 2006.

Stein, N. A'Yara. "It's All in the Translation." *Seeding the Snow*, Spring-Summer 2011.

Stewart, JT. "Ceremony." *Ceremony*. Sagittarius Press, 1990.

_____. "Say My Name." *Promised Lands: Poems from the Sovereign of Dishpan Sonnets*. Lamaya Press, 2010.

Taaffe, Sonya. "Matlacihuatl's Gift." *Dreams and Nightmares*, 63, 2002.

_____. "Madonna of the Cave." *Lone Star Stories*, 33, 2009.

Thomas, Sheree Renée. "untitled Old Scratch poem, featuring River." *Mythic*, 2, 2007.

Valente, Catherynne M. "The Girl with Two Skins." *Goblin Fruit*, Spring 2008.

_____. "The Oracle at Miami." *Oracles: A Pilgrimage*. Prime Press, 2005.

Vanderhooft, JoSelle. "The King's Daughters." *Fathers, Daughters, Ghosts, and Monsters*. vanZeno Press, 2009.

Victoria, Eliza. "Prayer." *Stone Telling*, 5, 2011.

Walton, Jo. "Blood Poem IV." *Goblin Fruit*, Summer 2006.

Wehle, Ellen. "Once I No Longer Lived Here." *Conjunctions*, Winter 2008.

Contributor Biographies

Mary Alexandra Agner writes of dead women, telescopes, and secrets in prose, poetry, and Ada. Her latest book is *The Scientific Method.* She can be found online at http://www.pantoum.org.

Sara Amis holds an MFA in Creative Writing from the University of Georgia and currently resides in Atlanta. Her work has appeared in *Magpie Magazine, The Dead Mule School of Southern Literature, Jabberwocky 3* and *5, Datura, Lilith: Queen of the Desert, Moon Milk Review, Southern Fried Weirdness: Reconstruction,* and *Right Hand Pointing.* Her poem series *The Sophia Leaves Text Messages* was published as a hand-bound limited edition by Papaveria Press, and she edits *Dead, Mad, or a Poet: A Journal to Faerie.*

Greek-born Athena Andreadis came to the US courtesy of full scholarships to Harvard, then MIT. She does basic research in molecular neurobiology, focusing on mechanisms of dementia. She is an avid reader in four languages, the author of *To Seek Out New Life: The Biology of Star Trek* and writes fiction and non-fiction on a wide swath of topics. Her work has appeared in *Harvard Review, Belles Lettres, Strange Horizons, Crossed Genres, Stone Telling, Cabinet des Fées, Bull Spec, Science in My Fiction, SF Signal, The Apex Blog, World SF, H+ Magazine,* and her own site, Starship Reckless at http://www.starshipreckless.com/.

Tara Barnett does not identify as a Native American, but is often questioned about her mixed heritage and looks. Her complicated relationship with her family's culture provided the background for "Star Reservation." She can be found online at http://tarabarnett.com.

Ari Berk is an award-winning writer, artist, and scholar. The former student of Pulitzer Prize-winning writer N. Scott Momaday, he has studied at Oxford and traveled widely, making friends in many parts of the world. He is the author of books for readers of all ages, including *The Runes of Elfland, Coyote Speaks — Wonders of the Native American World* (with Carolyn Dunn), and *The Secret Histories* series. His latest book is the much anticipated novel *Death Watch*, book one of The Undertaken Trilogy. His work has been translated into numerous languages. Dr. Berk is Professor of Mythology and Folklore at Central Michigan University and sits on the board of directors of the Mythic Imagination Institute. He lives in Michigan with his wife and son. To learn more about his work, visit him on the web at http://www.ariberk.com

Lisa Bradley's work has appeared in venues as diverse as *Mothering, Brutarian Quarterly, Cicada,* and *Weird Tales.* "The Haunted Girl" is the result of her complicated love for the horror genre, specifically the TV show *Supernatural.* "In Defiance of Sleek-Armed Androids" is just the result of complicated love. Originally from South Texas, Bradley now divides her time between Iowa and Exile, the setting of her novel-in-progress. One day, she'd like to live in New Mexico. She blogs at http://cafenowhere.livejournal.com.

Rachel Manija Brown has written poetry, books, television scripts, short stories, plays, video games, and comic books. Rachel's memoir *All the Fishes Come Home to Roost: An American Misfit in India* was published in nine countries and received rave reviews. She won third place in the Rhysling Awards for her poem "Nine Views of the Oracle." She is currently a student at Antioch University, working toward an MA in clinical psychology.

C.S.E. Cooney wishes it didn't cost 100 million dollars to travel to the moon. Until space travel is as common as the CTA, she'll just keep writing about it. Her fiction and poetry can be found at *Subterranean Press, Apex, Strange Horizons, Goblin Fruit,* and *Mythic Delirium.* Her novellas *The Big Bah-Ha* and *Jack o' the Hills* came out in early 2011 with Drollerie Press and Papaveria Press, respectively, and can be downloaded as e-books at Amazon.com. Her poetry collection *How to Flirt in Faerieland and Other Wild Rhymes* came out with Papaveria Press in April 2012.

Nandini Dhar's poems have appeared or are forthcoming in *Muse India, Kritya, Mascara Literary Review, Off the Coast, Pratilipi, tinfoildresses, First Literary Review, Poetry Quarterly, Stone Telling, Up the Staircase, Hawaii Review, Prick of the Spindle, lingerpost, Palooka, Inkscrawl, Chanterelle's Notebook, Cartographer: A Literary Review, Cabinet des Fees, Penwood Review,* and *Asia Writes.* A Pushcart nominee, Nandini grew up in Kolkata, India, and received an MA in Comparative Literature from Jadavpur University, Calcutta, and another MA in Comparative Literature from the University of Oregon. Currently, she is a PhD Candidate in Comparative Literature at University of Texas at Austin.

Kat Dixon is the author of the poetry-book *Temporary Yes* (Artistically Declined Press 2012). She comes dressed in yellow at http://isthiskatdixon.com.

Peg Duthie is a Taiwanese American native of Texas. In high school, a classmate threatened to spit on her because of her Mondale/Ferraro button. She now shares an old house in Tennessee with a small piano, a large dog, and a tall motorcycle mechanic. Her work has been anthologized in *Words of Power* (Phoenicia Publishing), *140 And Counting* (Upper Rubber Boot Books), *-gape-seed-* (Uphook Press), No Tell Motel's *Bedside Guides,* and elsewhere.

Amal El-Mohtar is a two-time winner of the Rhysling Award for Best Short Poem and has been nominated for the Nebula award. She is the author of *The Honey Month,* a collection of poetry and prose written to the taste of twenty-eight different kinds of honey. Her work has also appeared in *Apex, Strange Horizons, The Thackery T. Lambshead Cabinet of Curiosities,* and *Welcome to Bordertown,* and is forthcoming in *The Mammoth Book of Steampunk.* She also co-edits *Goblin Fruit,* an online quarterly dedicated to fantastical poetry, with Jessica P. Wick, and keeps a blog somewhat tidy at http://tithenai.livejournal.com.

Jeannelle M. Ferreira spends her days editing, believes in ghosts, and has been writing since she was five years old. She is the author of one novel, a two-mom-family children's book, a handful of short stories, and surprisingly, several poems. She is an accidental queer-parenting activist and an internet fiend. She received her undergraduate degree in creative writing from Brandeis University and lives in Maryland with her beloved wife and daughter. Jeannelle's work has most recently appeared in *Not One of Us #44*, *Stone Telling #4*, and *Steam-Powered II: More Lesbian Steampunk Stories*.

Greer Gilman's *Cloud & Ashes: Three Winter's Tales* won the 2010 Tiptree Award. Like her earlier novel *Moonwise*, it's set in a Northern mythscape, in a world where women turn the sky. Her Cloudish tales have also won a World Fantasy Award and a Crawford Award, and have been shortlisted for the Nebula and Mythopoeic Fantasy awards. Besides her two books, she has published other short work, poetry, and criticism. Her essay on "The Languages of the Fantastic" appears in *The Cambridge Companion to Fantasy Literature*. She likes to say she does everything James Joyce ever did, only backward and in high heels.

Theodora Goss was born in Hungary and spent her childhood in various European countries before her family moved to the United States. Although she grew up on the classics of English literature, her writing has been influenced by an Eastern European literary tradition in which the boundaries between realism and the fantastic are often ambiguous. Her publications include the short story collection *In the Forest of Forgetting* (2006); *Interfictions* (2007), a short story anthology coedited with Delia Sherman; and *Voices from Fairyland* (2008), a poetry anthology with critical essays and a selection of her own poems. Her short stories and poems have won the World Fantasy and Rhysling Awards.

Phyllis Gotlieb (1926-2009) was born and lived in Toronto all her life. She was happily married to computer scientist Calvin (Kelly) Gotlieb for 60 years and had 3 children and 4 grandchildren. Phyllis wrote 16 books — poetry and science fiction, and her works appear in more than a dozen languages. She was called the "grandmother of science fiction (or speculative fiction as she preferred to say) in Canada," and her awards include a Lifetime Achievement Award from SF Canada.

Their "Sunburst Award," the major juried Canadian SF award for the genre, is named after her first book. Her epitaph has the inscription "She graced this world, and imagined others."

Neile Graham is Canadian by birth and inclination, but currently lives in Seattle. Her poetry and fiction have been published in the US, the UK, and Canada, and she is a graduate of, and currently is workshop administrator for, Clarion West Writers Workshop. She has three full-length poetry collections: *Seven Robins* (1983), *Spells for Clear Vision* (1994), and *Blood Memory* (2000), and a spoken word CD, *She Says: Poems Selected and New* (2007/2009).

April Grant lives in Western Massachusetts, where she writes poetry and short fiction. At various times, she has worked as a restaurant hostess, librarian, and salesperson; she majored in history. Her humorous writing has appeared in *The Living Tradition*, and her poetry in *Strange Horizons*. One of her many ambitions is to travel internationally and fill the empty pages of her passport. Her literary influences include Christina Rossetti, Henry Austin Dobson, Freddy the Pig, Edith Nesbit, Archy the cockroach, and Phyllis McGinley.

Hel Gurney was born in rural Oxfordshire, studied English Language and Literature at King's College, London, and is now in Brighton pursuing postgraduate studies in representations of gender-transgression since the 16th century. Hel is fascinated by borders and binaries, memories and mythologies, and how they can be blurred and transcended. Appearing so far in *False Moustache* and *Stone Telling*, Hel's poetry roams across time, space, and genre. A committed activist, Hel also operates queer-feminist promotions label "The Cutlery Drawer," organizing events that showcase marginalized artists and fundraise for causes related to gender and sexuality. http://helgurney.wordpress.com

Minal Hajratwala is the author of *Leaving India: My Family's Journey from Five Villages to Five Continents* (Houghton Mifflin Harcourt, 2009), which won a Pen USA Award, an Asian American Writers Workshop Award, a Lambda Literary Award, and a California Book Award. She is the editor of *Out: Stories from the New Queer India*, forthcoming in 2012 from Queer Ink Publishing. Her one-woman show, "Avatars: Gods for a New Millennium," was commissioned by the Asian Art Museum of San Francisco for World AIDS Day in 1999. Currently, Ms. Hajratwala is researching a novel and writing poems about the unicorns of the 5,000-year-old Indus Valley civilization. For more information, please visit http://www.minalhajratwala.com/.

Samantha Henderson is from Southern California by way of England, South Africa, Illinois, and Oregon. Her poetry has been published in *Goblin Fruit, Strange Horizons, Weird Tales, Stone Telling*, and *Mythic Delirium*, and she is the co-winner of the 2010 Rhysling Award for speculative poetry. She would like to thank her mother-in-law for the berry cobbler recipe.

The daughter of Chinese-American immigrants, Emily Jiang was born in California and raised in Texas. A graduate of the Clarion Writers' Workshop in San Diego, Emily has a BA in English from Rice University and an MFA in Creative Writing from Saint Mary's College of California, where she wrote "Self-Portrait." Her poetry has been published in *Stone Telling, Strange Horizons*, and *Goblin Fruit*. She wrestles with words every day. Sometimes she wins. Most times, it's a draw.

C. W. Johnson has a bachelor's degree in math and a PhD in theoretical physics. He has published ten stories, twenty poems, and over thirty scientific articles. He lives somewhere in California.

Meena Kandasamy is a poet, writer, activist, and translator. Her work maintains a focus on caste annihilation, linguistic identity, and feminism. She has published two collections of poetry: *Touch* (2006) and *Ms Militancy* (2010). Currently, she is a Charles Wallace India Trust Fellow at the School of English, University of Kent, Canterbury, UK. Two of her poems, "Mascara" and "My Lover Speaks of Rape," have won first prizes in pan-India poetry competitions, and her poetry has been profiled in several international publications. Previously, she edited *The Dalit*, a bi-monthly English magazine.

Nicole Kornher-Stace's short fiction and poetry have appeared or are forthcoming in a number of magazines and anthologies, including *Best American Fantasy*, *Clockwork Phoenix 3*, *The Mammoth Book of Steampunk*, *Apex*, and *Fantasy Magazine*. Her work has placed 2nd in the Rhysling Awards and been longlisted for the British Fantasy Awards and nominated for the Pushcart Prize. She is the author of *Desideria*, *Demon Lovers and Other Difficulties*, and *The Winter Triptych*. Her current novel-in-progress is a blend of steampunk and mythpunk, with a Lady Explorer, a fake Tarot, a workers' rebellion, a demon-possessed airship, and other miscellany. She can be found online at http://nicolekornherstace.com or http://wirewalking.livejournal.com.

As of 2011, Ursula K. Le Guin has published twenty-one novels, eleven volumes of short stories, four collections of essays, twelve books for children, six volumes of poetry, and four of translation, and has received many awards: Hugo, Nebula, National Book Award, PEN-Malamud, etc. Her recent publications include the novel *Lavinia*, an essay collection, *Cheek by Jowl*, and *The Wild Girls*. Forthcoming in 2012, *Finding My Elegy, New and Selected Poems*. She lives in Portland, Oregon.

Yoon Ha Lee's poetry has appeared in *Strange Horizons*, *Mythic Delirium*, and *Jabberwocky*. She lives in Louisiana with her family.

Alex Dally MacFarlane lives and works in London, where she soon plans to return to academia. Her work has appeared or is forthcoming in *The Mammoth Book of Steampunk*, *Steam-Powered 2: More Lesbian Steampunk Stories*, *Clarkesworld Magazine*, *Fantasy Magazine*, *EscapePod*, *Sybil's Garage*, and *Goblin Fruit*, and has been nominated for the Rhysling Award. A handbound limited edition of her story "Two Coins" was published by Papaveria Press in 2010. She keeps a website at http://alexdallymacfarlane.com.

Rebecca Marjesdatter is the poetry editor for *Tales of the Unanticipated*, a Rhysling winner and member of the performance group Lady Poetesses from Hell. She lives in Minneapolis, Minnesota.

Jennifer A. McGowan attended Princeton University, graduating *cum laude*, and obtained her MA and PhD from the University of Wales. Despite being certified as disabled at age 16 with Ehlers-Danlos Syndrome, she went on to become a semi-professional mime and performed in five countries before the disability became too much. She has published poetry and prose in many magazines and anthologies including *The Connecticut Review*, *Envoi*, and *Acumen*, and has both written and recorded songs on several labels. *Life in Captivity*, her chapbook, is available from Finishing Line Press. Having been resident in the UK since 1992, she recently naturalized. Her website can be found at http://www.jenniferamcgowan.com.

Elizabeth R. McClellan is a third-year law student and Rhysling-nominated poet who lives in a probably-haunted apartment house in Memphis, Tennessee. Her work has appeared in *Apex Magazine*, *Goblin Fruit*, *The Legendary*, and *Stone Telling*. Her work is forthcoming in the *I Know What I Saw* anthology edited by Barry Napier. McClellan remembers pitching half a fit in the movie theater when she saw what Disney had done to Andersen's *The Little Mermaid*. Having used GLaDOS' voice to induce stress conditions while preparing for the LSAT, she has a particular soft spot for that psychotic AI. McClellan hopes that her scholarly work promoting the viability of legal personhood for artificial intelligence will keep her safe when the computers take over, if only for a little while.

Sharon Mock's short stories have appeared in *Realms of Fantasy*, *Clarkesworld Magazine*, and *Fantasy Magazine*, among others. Her poems can be found in *Astrapoetica*, *Comets and Criminals*, and *Mythic Delerium*. She lives in Southern California, and would be a marine biologist in an alternate life.

Patricia Monaghan is the author of four books of poetry including the recent *Homefront*, which explores the impact of war on families. She has also written more than a dozen nonfiction books: two encyclopediae of myths including *The Encyclopedia of Goddesses and Heroines*; a spiritual geography of Ireland entitled *The Red-Haired Girl from the Bog*; a book on gardening called *Magical Gardens*; and other titles in spirituality and feminism. She is professor of interdisciplinary studies at DePaul University in Chicago and Senior Fellow at the Black Earth Institute in Wisconsin.

Koel Mukherjee grew up in the south of England and a twisty-laned town near Kolkata, where an unquantifiable portion of her heart still lives. The rest of her lives in a small, sunny flat in South London where she writes poetry about disobedient boats and mythological characters with gumption. Koel has an MA in Asian History from the School of Oriental and African Studies, and her current fixations are undeciphered scripts, *The West Wing*, and whether or not to plunge into the joy and terror of a PhD. "Sita Reflects" is her first published poem.

Ranjani Murali graduated from George Mason University with an MFA in poetry. Her poetry, translations and prose have appeared in *elimae, Indefinite Space, Kartika Review, Asia Writes, Phoebe*, and *Cricket Online Review*. She received the Kay Evans Fellowship from the Vermont Studio Center for a poetry residency. She lives in Chicago and volunteers as an ESL tutor.

Kristine Ong Muslim has short fiction and poetry appearing in hundreds of publications, including *Abyss & Apex, Eschatology, Expanded Horizons, Paper Crow, Polluto, Space & Time*, and *Tales of the Talisman*. She authored *Night Fish* (Shoe Music Press/Elevated Books) and *Smaller than Most* (Philistine Press). She has been nominated five times for the Pushcart Prize and four times for the Science Fiction Poetry Association's Rhysling Award.

Shweta Narayan was born in India and has lived in Malaysia, Saudi Arabia, the Netherlands, Scotland, and California. Her poetry and fiction often feature outsiders, people on the margins. "Cave-Smell" isn't as directly autobiographical as "Epiphyte" is, but there are bits of her life in both. Shweta's poetry can also be found in *Goblin Fruit, Stone Telling*, and *Strange Horizons*, and her fiction in places like *Strange Horizons, the Beastly Bride* anthology, and *Steampunk II: Steampunk Reloaded*. Her novelette "Pishaach" was a Nebula Award nominee.

Shweta was the Octavia E. Butler Memorial Scholarship recipient at the 2007 Clarion workshop.

Adrienne J. Odasso was born in Cleveland, Ohio, and raised in Brookville, Pennsylvania. Her poetry has appeared in a variety of publications, including *Sybil's Garage, Farrago's Wainscot, Fear and Trembling, Mythic Delirium, Jabberwocky, Cabinet des Fées, Midnight Echo, Not One of Us, Dreams & Nightmares*, and *Goblin Fruit* (just to name a few). Her two chapbooks, *Devil's Road Down* and *Wanderlust*, are currently available from Maverick Duck Press. Her first full collection, *Lost Books*, was released in April 2010 by Flipped Eye Publishing. She lives in London with her husband, James.

Kelly Rose Pflug-Back is a twenty-two-year-old writer, student, and social activist whose poetry and fiction have been published in places like *Mythic Delirium, Ideomancer, This Magazine*, and *Not One of Us*. She often uses speculative, fantastical, and horrific imagery to address real-world issues, both current and historical. She also writes non-fiction about queer and transgender issues, international feminism, social justice, and (dis)ability politics. When she isn't struggling to form coherent sentences from her many chaotic thoughts, she likes to paint, do volunteer work, and make music.

Cassandra Phillips-Sears' short fiction and poetry have appeared in *Goblin Fruit, Scheherezade's Bequest, Jabberwocky 2, Not One of Us, Place/Time, Sirenia Digest*, and in the collection *A Field Guide to Surreal Botany* by Two Cranes Press. She lives in Massachusetts. To find out more, please visit her website, http://eredien.livejournal.com.

Sofía Rhei has published various books of poetry, including *Alicia volátil* (El Cangrejo Pistolero), *Las flores del alcohol* (La Bella Varsovia), *Versiones* (Ediciones del primor), *Química* (El Gaviero), and *Las ciudades reversibles* (Colegio de Arquitectos de Ciudad Real). Her most recent novel is the YA fantasy *Flores de sombra* (Alfaguara). English translations of her poems have appeared in *Strange Horizons, Space & Time, Mythic Delirium, STAR*LINE, Pank*, and other magazines. Her website is http://www.sofiarhei.com.

Sally Rosen Kindred's first full-length poetry collection is *No Eden* (Mayapple Press, 2011). Her poems have appeared in *Blackbird* and on *Verse Daily*, and are forthcoming in *Quarterly West* and *Hunger Mountain*. Her awards include fellowships from the Maryland State Arts Council and the Virginia Center for Creative Arts.

J. C. Runolfson's work has appeared in *Goblin Fruit, Mythic Delirium, Strange Horizons*, and *Stone Telling*, among others. She is also an outspoken critic who reviews both speculative poetry and prose for various venues, and is dedicated to promoting a diversity of voices and perspectives in the field. She can be found nattering on about these topics, as well as her four beloved dogs, online at her blog, http://seajules.livejournal.com.

Ki Russell is currently a doctoral candidate in the University of Louisiana at Lafayette's English department. She also serves as poetry co-editor of *Rougarou: An Online Literary Journal*. Outside of academia, Ki has a wonderful son and husband who put up with her eccentricities with pretty good humor. She often steals time from sludging through academic drear to wrestle with words, converse with a gray cat, and paint. She also believes people should laugh more. Her work has appeared in places such as *Fifth Wednesday Journal, Electric Velocipede, Rio Grande Review, Sugar House Review, Etchings* (Australia), and other journals.

Sofia Samatar is an American of Somali and Swiss-German Mennonite background. She has lived in Egypt and South Sudan, and is currently pursuing a doctorate in African Languages and Literature at the University of Wisconsin–Madison, where she specializes in 20th-century Egyptian and Sudanese literatures. Her poetry has appeared in *Stone Telling* and *Bull Spec*, and her debut novel, *A Stranger in Olondria*, will be published by Small Beer Press in 2012.

Lorraine Schein is a New York poet and writer. Her poetry has appeared in *Gargoyle, Vallum, New Letters, Strange Horizons, Sagewoman, Witches & Pagans, Women's Studies Quarterly*, the *We'Moon* calendar, and elsewhere. Her fiction and humor are included in the anthologies *The Unbearables, Wild Women,* and *Alice Redux,* an anthology about Alice in Wonderland. *The Futurist's Mistress,* her poetry book, is available from Mayapple Press. She is currently working on a graphic novel.

Lawrence Schimel has published over 100 books, including the poetry collection *Fairy Tales for Writers* and the forthcoming anthology *Flamboyant: A Celebration of Jewish Gay Poetry* (both A Midsummer Night's Press). He won the Rhysling Award for his poem "How to Make a Human" and has also won the Lambda Literary Award (for *PoMosexuals: Challenging Assumptions about Gender and Sexuality* (Cleis) and for *First Person Queer* (Arsenal Pulp)), and the Spectrum Award for *The Future Is Queer* (Arsenal Pulp), among other prizes. He lives in Madrid, Spain, where he works as a Spanish->English translator.

Nisi Shawl's *Filter House* won the 2009 James Tiptree, Jr. Award. Shawl is one of the founders of the Carl Brandon Society, and is co-author of *Writing the Other: A Practical Approach.* She edited *The WisCon Chronicles, Vol. 5: Writing and Racial Identity. Something More and More,* a collection celebrating her WisCon 35 Guest of Honor status, appeared in May 2011. "Transbluency" was first published in the June/July issue of *Stone Telling.* Her poem "To Jack Kerouac, to Make Much of Space and Time" is included in the epistolary anthology *Talking Back.* She blogs on LiveJournal, and hopes to update her website soon.

Delia Sherman is best known as a writer of short stories and novels. Her short fiction has appeared in many anthologies, most recently *Teeth* and *Naked City.* Her most recent novels are for younger readers: *Changeling* and *The Magic Mirror of the Mermaid Queen* and the forthcoming *The Freedom Maze.* She does not think of herself as a poet, but will write it when someone (in this case, Terri Windling) tells her to. When not gallivanting hither and yon, she lives in New York City with her wife, Ellen Kushner, many books, and no pets whatsoever.

Vandana Singh was born and raised in India and currently lives near Boston, where she teaches physics at a state university and writes mostly short stories and some poetry. Her work has appeared in numerous anthologies and magazines and has been reprinted in several recent Year's Best volumes. One of her poems once made second place in the Rhysling awards. Her Aqueduct Press novella *Distances* won the Carl Brandon Parallax Award for 2008 and was a Tiptree Honor book. For more about her, please see her website at http://users.rcn.com/singhvan and her blog at http://vandanasingh.wordpress.com/.

N. A'Yara Stein is a Romani-American poet and writer who has been nominated twice for the 2010 Pushcart Prize by *Apparatus Magazine* and *Vox Poetica*. She holds an MFA from the University of Arkansas and is a grant recipient of the Michigan Art Council and the Arkansas Arts Council, among other honors. The former editor of the arts quarterly *Gypsy Blood Review*, she's recently published in *Verse Wisconsin*, *The Mayo Review*, *Ping Pong: The Journal of the Henry Miller Library*, *The Chaffey Review*, *The San Pedro Poetry Review*, *The Delinquent, UK*, among others. She lives near Chicago with her sons, is looking for a book publisher, and is the featured poet in the spring/summer 2011 issue of *The James Dickey Review*.

JT Stewart claims these specialties: poet, writer, playwright, editor, teacher. She gets a warm glow about these achievements: Co-Founder of the Clarion West SF Writers' Workshop and Poetry Editor for *Seattle Poets & Photographers: A Millennium Reflection* (University of Washington Press). As a woman of African descent, she often writes about cultural collisions and the fortunes/misfortunes of people touched by diasporas — both real and imagined. As a public artist, JT specializes in poetry broadsides of all sizes. She has had her work placed at Western Washington University, the Seattle Art Museum, and the Allen Library at the University of Washington.

Poems and short stories by Sonya Taaffe have won the Rhysling Award, been shortlisted for the SLF Fountain Award and the Dwarf Stars Award, and been reprinted in *The Year's Best Fantasy and Horror*, *The Alchemy of Stars: Rhysling Award Winners Showcase*, *The*

Best of Not One of Us, and *Trochu divné kusy 3.* A selection of her work has been collected in *Postcards from the Province of Hyphens,* *Singing Innocence and Experience* (Prime Books), and *A Mayse-Bikhl* (Papaveria Press). She is presently on the editorial staff of *Strange Horizons*; she holds masters' degrees in Classics from Brandeis and Yale and once named a Kuiper belt object.

Memphian Sheree Renée Thomas first read Octavia E. Butler's *Kindred* in a slavery and literature class at Rhodes. She later studied at NYU's Publishing program and the Frederick Douglass Creative Arts Center in Manhattan. With the support of phenomenal women mentors in publishing, Thomas edited fiction, copyedited manuscripts, and wrote jacket copy, an invaluable experience that helped hone her skills and reimagine her creative vision. Her Dark Matter black speculative fiction anthologies were named *New York Times* Notable Book of the Year (2000) and honored with the 2001 and 2005 World Fantasy Award. A '99 Clarion West alum, where she studied with Greg Bear, Octavia E. Butler, Gwyneth Jones, Nancy Kress, and Gordon Van Gelder, Sheree is the author of *Shotgun Lullabies: Stories & Poems,* published by Aqueduct Press.

Catherynne M. Valente is a *New York Times* bestselling author of over a dozen works of fiction and poetry, including *Palimpsest,* the *Orphan's Tales* series, *Deathless,* and the crowdfunded phenomenon *The Girl Who Circumnavigated Fairyland in a Ship of Her Own Making.* She is the winner of the Tiptree Award, the Mythopoeic Award, the Rhysling Award, and the Million Writers Award. She has been nominated for the Hugo, Locus, and Spectrum Awards, the Pushcart Prize, and was a finalist for the World Fantasy Award in 2007 and 2009. She lives on an island off the coast of Maine with her partner, two dogs, and an enormous cat.

JoSelle Vanderhooft is the author of several poetry collections, including *Fathers, Daughters, Ghosts & Monsters* (vanZeno Press, 2009) and the 2008 Bram Stoker Award finalist *Ossuary* (Sam's Dot Publishing, 2007). She is the editor of several anthologies including *Steam-*

Powered: Lesbian Steampunk Stories and (with Catherine Lundoff) *Hellebore & Rue: Tales of Lesbian Magic Users.* She lives in Florida.

Eliza Victoria lives in the Philippines. Her fiction and poetry have appeared in various publications, including *Stone Telling, The Pedestal Magazine, High Chair, Story Quarterly*, and the *Philippine Speculative Fiction* series. Visit her at http://sungazer.wordpress.com.

Jo Walton is a science fiction and fantasy writer. She has published two poetry collections and nine novels, most recently *Among Others.* She has won the John W. Campbell Award, the World Fantasy Award, the Prometheus Award, and the Mythopoeic Award. She comes from Wales but lives in Montreal where the food and books are much better.

Ellen Wehle is a reviewer and contributing editor at *West Branch.* Her poetry collection *The Ocean Liner's Wake* came out from Shearsman Books in 2009, and she is presently completing her first novel.

Editor Biography

Rose Lemberg lived on the Ukrainian/Polish border, in subarctic Russia, and in Israel before moving to the US to become a graduate student at UC Berkeley. Some years later she defended her dissertation and moved to the Midwest, where she at last officially became an immigrant. She works as an assistant professor at a local university. Her short stories have appeared in *Strange Horizons, Fantasy Magazine, Beneath Ceaseless Skies*, and other venues, and her poetry in *Goblin Fruit, Apex, Strange Horizons,* and other venues. Her queer epic poem "In the Third Cycle" won the Rannu competition in 2011. She is the founder and co-editor (with Shweta Narayan) of *Stone Telling,* a magazine of boundary-crossing speculative poetry. Rose and Shweta are committed to nurturing diversity within the speculative poetry field, and much of the work they publish is feminist. Rose is looking forward to many more adventures in feminist literature of the fantastic. She can be found online at http://roselemberg.net.